THE LAST STOP

Great explorers love Polar Bear Press

DISAPPEARING ONTARIO
by Ron Brown
Images from our vanishing countryside

GHOST RAILWAYS OF ONTARIO VOL. I & II
by Ron Brown
Explore Ontario's forgotten train stations, roundhouses and railroads

GHOST TOWNS OF ONTARIO: A field guide VOL. I & II
by Ron Brown
Ghost towns to explore, how they came to be and where to find them

HAUNTED ONTARIO
by Terry Boyle
Ghostly inns, hotels and other eerie places you can visit

HIDDEN ONTARIO
by Terry Boyle
Secrets of the past

FULL MOONS & BLACK CATS
by Terry Boyle
Everyday Rules to Guide Your Life

ONTARIO'S VANISHED VILLAGES
by Ron Brown
Discover whistlestops, old mills, lost hamlets, relics and ruins of Ontario

TORONTO'S LOST VILLAGES
by Ron Brown
Discover a Toronto you never knew

CASTLES & KINGS
by Ron Brown
Ontario Mansions and the People Who Lived in Them

FIT TO BE TIED
by Terry Boyle
Ontario's Murderous Past

NOTES ON A BEERMAT
by Nicholas Pashley
Drinking and Why It's Necessary

THE LAST STOP

Ontario's heritage railway stations

RON BROWN

Polar Bear Press, Toronto

Special thanks to Parks Canada, Heritage Canada,
for their considerable assistance in this project.

Polar
Bear
Press

Distributed by
North 49 Books
35 Prince Andrew Place
Toronto, Ontario
M3C 2H2
(416) 449-4000

National Library of Canada Canadian Cataloguing in Publication Data

Brown Ron, 1945-
  The last stop : Ontario's heritage railway stations

ISBN 1-896757-19-7

1. Railroad stations—Ontario—History. 2. Historic sites Ontario-Guidebooks. 3. Ontario-Guidebooks. 1. Title.

TF302.05SB76 2002   385.3114109713
C2002-900801-8   385.314

2002 03 04 10 9 8 7 6 5 4 3 2 1

Printed in Canada

Canada

"We acknowledge the financial support of the Government of Canada through the Book Publishing Industry Development Program for this project."

TABLE OF CONTENTS

INTRODUCTION

On November 22, 1982, Toronto Mayor Arthur Eggleton was roused from his breakfast by an urgent call. The West Toronto CP station had been demolished overnight. Despite months of negotiation involving the City, the West Toronto Junction Historical Society and the CPR, the station was rubble. A furious Eggleton confronted the wrecking crew, but it was too late. The remaining bricks and stones were piled onto waiting freight cars and highballed to a dump near MacTier.

It was the wake-up call which railway heritage enthusiasts in Ontario needed. Despite the steady removal of stations in towns right across the province, there had been little co-ordinated effort to save them. Provincial heritage laws were toothless to affect buildings covered by a federal railway act. Railway stations by the thousands had become redundant and railway companies refused to recognize their heritage value. During the hearings which followed the West Toronto demolition, one CP lawyer dismissed the station as a "boarded-up shack." If Ontario's stations were to be saved, a miracle had to come out of Ottawa. And that miracle worker would be the MP for the riding of Parkdale, in which the doomed station had stood, Jesse Flis.

Two years after the secretive demolition, Flis introduced a private members' bill which would not only prevent the demolition of designated stations, but require a thorough review before any alterations could occur. Another four years would pass, however, before the bill finally received royal assent.

The legislation allows eligible stations, that is those in railway ownership, to be reviewed by the Minister of the Environment and, possibly designated.

The criteria used to evaluate the stations include:

- age (50 years or older is preferred),
- significance of the station's history,
- how well the station illustrates the development of the community,
- aesthetic or visual quality of the station,
- functional and technical quality,
- relationship between the station and the area with which it is associated, and
- nature of the station's identity within that community.

While nearly every station which still stands could easily be labelled a "heritage" station, the focus of this book is solely upon those designated by this federal legislation. These stations are those which remain closest to their roots. At the time of designation they remained in railway ownership and stood on active railway lines. Some still served passengers, others simply sheltered maintenance crews. Since designation a few have entered into new uses. Without Jesse Flis and his law, most of them would have long since had their "last stop."

At one time more than three thousand stations stood in Ontario. These ranged from flag stop shelters to the way stations which marked the heart of small town Ontario to the grand urban terminals which were often the finest buildings in the cities. Everything went by train, from milk and mail to livestock, manufactured goods, gold, silver and even precious silk. People flocked to the station to await long-lost relatives, or to bid farewell to loved ones, never knowing when they would see them again. Between trains, folks gathered there to dance, play cards or listen to the hockey scores come in on the news wire.

The architecture of stations reflected this role. In the beginning stations were often hastily-erected wooden shacks, or were plunked into existing buildings. Then, once the trains began to turn a profit, the railway companies could turn to aesthetics. Many of North America's leading architects were hired to create elaborate station buildings. Arches, pillars, towers and conical rooves known as witch's hats soon decorated the local stations. Between the two wars, when rail traffic slowed, station styles became simpler. The modern age which followed World War II brought with it more modern stations. In an attempt to revive its flagging passenger traffic, the CPR introduced not just streamlined stations, but streamlined trains as well.

Where new stations were required, they often reflected a nostalgia for the older stations. While the new Ottawa station, built in the 1960s, revisited the train shed, the station in London Ontario, which opened in 2001, brought back the tower and the vaulted waited room.

The decline of the railway era began after World War I. Because of the crushing debt of the war, government funding of railways dried up and several railway lines went bankrupt. Redundant lines were removed. The auto age arrived and passengers began to abandon the trains for the flexibility of the car. From the 1950s and '60s transcontinental flights could whisk Canadians across their country in five hours, rather than the five days in a train. The end of steam, the introduction of automated traffic control, and the elimination of local freight service all made thousands of stations redundant. During the 1970s and '80s, more than 90% of Ontario's stations were removed.

It took the new Heritage Railway Station Protection Act (HRSP) to halt the wholesale removal of Ontario's heritage stations. Several attempts prior to the tough new law had limited success. The Ontario Ministry of Citizenship and Culture had commissioned a two-volume assessment of Ontario's "heritage" stations but could offer no way to save them. The Ontario Ministry of Transportation and Communication provided funds to convert stations to multi-modal terminals, but because of the cost, few were affected. The Ministry of Municipal Affairs' PRIDE program allowed the Town of Rainy River to purchase its unique Canadian Northern station and convert it to community use. More recently, and in a welcome change of attitude, CP itself has established a heritage fund designed to protect and celebrate buildings which relate to that historic line. In Ontario, two stations to receive such funding are the stations from Wolverton and Smiths' Falls.

Since Flis's bill was enacted, more than 50 stations in Ontario have received a federal heritage designation and are protected from alteration or demolition. Nevertheless, this number remains a small portion of the more than 250 stations which survive in Ontario. There are several excellent references which focus upon them such as Elizabeth Wilmot's nostalgic railway station trilogy *Meet Me At the Station*, *Faces and Places Along the Railway*, and *When Anytime was Train Time*. The most comprehensive work to date is that edited by Bruce Ballantyne and published by the Bytown Railway Society, the *Canadian Railway Station Guide*.

That so many non-designated stations were rescued is due to the dedicated work of community groups across Ontario. Thanks to these concerned citizens, stations by the scores have become libraries, restaurants, museums and private homes.

Still, without the teeth of this protective legislation, active railway stations would have been doomed. The federal act has allowed Ontario to hang onto a piece of its heritage that was very nearly allowed to vanish from its landscape. This book celebrates that victory.

The beautiful Tudor-style West Toronto station whose demolition launched the drive to legislate protection for Canada's heritage railway stations.

Despite being designated, the once pretty St Clair station in Toronto could not be rescued from vandalism and ultimately arson.

ALEXANDRIA
The Trudeau Train

Although many Canadians may not realize it, they have seen the Alexandria station. During the televised coverage of Pierre Trudeau's funeral train, TV cameras captured the moving image of flag-waving crowds clustered about the platform of the Alexandria railway station as Trudeau's sons, Sacha and Michel, leaned to greet them.

Like that at Orillia, the station in Alexandria was a war time pro-

Many Canadians saw the Alexandria station during the TV coverage of Pierre Trudeau's funeral train.

ject. It was constructed in 1917, replacing the original Canada Atlantic Railway station, to facilitate the movement of troops and supplies to Halifax and then overseas. Although it was not a large building, the higher roofline over the ticket office and bay gave it a decidedly "grand" aspect.

Like most small town stations, it was divided into three functional areas, the freight and baggage area on the east end, the waiting room on the west, with the ticket office and operator's office between. And, like so many others, the CAR had located its line well to the north of the town, thus avoiding higher land costs.

Prior to the war, many industries had located around the station, including warehouses, factories and livestock pens. Behind the station a handsome brick hotel provided meals and rooms for the travellers.

Following the second war, with the rise in shipment by trucks, the station lost its significance in moving freight and many of the industries moved away, leaving only a warehouse and grain elevator. The hotel still survives and still provides refreshment to the public, although few of these are train travellers.

Since VIA assumed rail passenger service here in 1983, it has altered the waiting area and improved handicap access. CN no longer operates from the station, and the building is now leased to a local travel agent who provides service on behalf of VIA. The station, which lies halfway along the Montreal to Ottawa corridor, sees nine trains call each day. It is situated on McDougald Street, off Main Street and well to the north of the main part of town.

ALLANDALE (BARRIE)
Ontario's Largest Wooden Station

One of Ontario's most eclectic and visually distinctive railway stations is that which the Grand Trunk built at Allandale, now part of Barrie. Its separate functions appeared as literally three different buildings, and extended a considerable distance along the curving track.

Ontario's first railway line, the Ontario Simcoe and Huron, reached the shores of Lake Simcoe in 1853, and established the location as a divisional point. As the Northern Railway, the line was extended to Collingwood to the northwest, and several years later, as

The Allandale station before the tracks were lifted and neglect set in.

the Western and Pacific Junction Railway to Gravenhurst and Callander to the northeast.

The small board and batten building ticked into the V of the junction was proving to be too small and in 1905 the Grand Trunk, as part of its national upgrading plan, chose to replace it. It hired the Detroit firm of Spier and Rohns, famous for the towered stations they had designed for the Grand Trunk in Michigan, and for that in Brantford, to design the new structure.

Adopting their favourite Italianate theme, the architects formulated a wooden waiting room, agents' office and baggage area with a rounded bay on the south so that travellers could not only see the train movements, but also enjoy a view of the scenic Kempenfeldt Bay which spread out in front of the station. A crown-like canopy decorated the window line. A large square two storey bay window stood on the eastern side, topped by a tall observation tower. A series of gables added interest to the roof line.

Next in line was the restaurant, likewise constructed of wood.

VIA Rail's *Canadian* makes one of its last stops at the Allandale station.

Connected by a pillared breezeway to the waiting room, it is distinguished by a series of tall pillars on its eastern entrance, through which most of the passengers arrived. But this was not the simple lunch counter usually found at divisional stations. Many of its patrons, after all, were wealthy cottage owners travelling by train and steamer to their ample summer homes on Muskoka Lake. Rather, with seating for 50 and a bar area for 60 more, the restaurant used uniformed staff, and boasted a Grand Hall design with carved wainscotting and simulated beams "supported" by paired columns into which were carved the letters GTR. Tall windows provided ample lighting as well as views over Kempenfeldt Bay.

The third structure, a two storey brick office building, likewise connected with a breezeway, had been built five years previously. Between them, the three buildings stretched more than two hundred feet along the curving track.

Allandale, although not company owned, was nonetheless a true railway town. The yards spread out to the east of the station where a mechanics shop, engine shop and large roundhouse were situated. Housing developed south of the tracks, while industry lined up northwest of the station. In addition, the YMCA located one of their railway Y's close to the station, where train crews awaiting their return shift could relax with a book or sleep in a warm bed.

The 1950s marked the beginning of a new era for the station and its town. Under the CNR, the divisional point was closed, and staff relocated to Capreol. The dining room was remodelled into a soda bar with a pair of counters replacing chairs and tables, its high ceiling covered over. The roof line was simplified, the tower and the crown canopy being removed.

By the 1980s more changes came. The waiting room and restaurant were closed and passengers relocated into the brick office building where the smaller number of railway staff now used the upper floor. Most of the yard tracks were lifted, and the ancillary buildings, with one notable exception, removed. Then, in the 1990s, the office itself closed, and a small aluminum shed erected to accommodate the VIA ticket agent and waiting passengers.

Today, the entire complex stands vacant and overgrown with weeds. In 1997, CN lifted the tracks from the front of the station forcing VIA to re-route its trains around the much less populated eastern side of Lake Simcoe. The line to Collingwood, still in place to the west of the station, has been operated as a short line railway owned by the City of Barrie. Along the shoreline, tracks have been replaced with a roadway and parkland. Of all the yard buildings only the former mechanics shop has survived. It has been declared a locally significant heritage building and renovated to house a banquet facility and information office. The one-time Y became a popular tavern and restaurant.

But as for the remarkable Allandale station itself, the future is much less certain. Despite the hard work of Heritage Barrie, a citizens' group, the City of Barrie carries a less than stellar record of preserving historic buildings. It has, however, shown concern over the Allandale station, having purchased the building along with CN's trackage for the Barrie-Collingwood Railway operation. Although a number of private proposals have come and gone, the building remains vacant. Still, it stands as one of the most prominent landmarks along Barrie's ample lakeshore, and remains one of Ontario's most striking stations.

AURORA
Ontario's First Station Stop

The recently renovated station at Aurora combines a legacy of appearance, siting and history, making it one of the region's most significant heritage railway stations.

It is not, however, the oldest, nor is it the largest or most elaborate.

But Ontario's railway history began here. In June of 1853, a diminutive steam engine hissed to a halt amid the farms and forests near what was then the hamlet of Machel's Corners. This historic run marked the first steam railway operation in the province and would

Now restored, the historic Aurora station is a busy GO station.

launch a five decade binge of railway building, a flurry which would turn Ontario's countryside into a spider's web of railway lines.

The first station was built to a simple board and batten pattern. The style was employed by the Ontario Simcoe and Huron Railway (Oats Straw and Hay to its detractors), at like-sized communities between Toronto and Barrie. The placing of the station east of Yonge Street drew the village's growth in that direction and within a few years the rail line marked eastern boundary of the newly renamed Aurora. Factories, a water tower and other ancillary buildings soon surrounded the station, and a railway hotel was added a short distance north.

By 1900, however, the Grand Trunk, which had just taken over 49 small railway lines, including the OSH, was launching its extensive program of track upgrades and station replacements. If it was to keep ahead of its aggressive rival, the CPR, the GT had to regain its prominence in the region. By then Ontario's pioneer railway had extended its tentacles to Collingwood on Georgian Bay and through Muskoka to Lake Nipissing as well. By the time CN had taken over Canada's many bankrupt lines, Aurora found itself on a cross-Canada main line.

The style used in Aurora was known as the Stick Style. It placed visual emphasis upon the framing of the building, such as cross braces and vertical and horizontal framing. Originally, the station included gables at each end as well as over the operator's bay window. The fretwork within them resembled a sunburst. That at the north end in fact extended to cover a porte-cochere mounted upon slim wooden pillars. The intricate carving within the gables was an exceptional feature of the Aurora station, but was one which was repeated in other stick style stations such as those at Newmarket and Maple.

At first, the interior had waiting rooms at the north and south ends with the ticket office and agent's area between. Later, around 1930, a freight area was added to the south end eliminating the original gable. Unfortunately, many of the exterior features of the stick style were also covered over with grey insulbrick.

By the 1970s train traffic was dwindling, and many of the railway buildings were removed. GO Transit then began service to the town, resulting in still more alterations. At the same time wood rot had begun to set in and the station was showing serious signs of deterioration. Spurred on by a heritage conscious community, GO Transit began a major restoration of the Aurora station. While the interior was altered to accommodate GO travellers, the stick style exterior was fully revealed and repainted. The freight shed extension was removed and the south end restored as well. The station hotel has managed to survive as a residence, and in small part helps to enhance the diminished railway landscape.

The rail line still defines the east end of the town's residential area, where a flurry of excitement erupts each evening with the return of daily commuters. Unfortunately, few other trains pass this way. In 1997, the CN suddenly removed its tracks between Barrie and Orillia, utterly severing the southern portion of this historic line with the main line.

The Aurora station is on the south side of Wellington St, several blocks east of Yonge St, the village's historical main commercial street.

The Aurora station as it was originally constructed.

BELLEVILLE
Just a Waiting Room

When is a station not a station? The answer: when it is simply a waiting room. By most definitions, railway stations combined a variety of functions including the handling of passengers and their baggage, usually freight, and the operation of train movements. From the beginning, the two-storey stone station at Belleville was never anything more than just a waiting room.

That beginning dates from 1856 when the Grand Trunk Railway began running trains on its vital new Toronto to Montreal main line.

The Belleville station displays its distinctive mansard roof.

Plans called for 34 stone or brick stations built to similar styles on the route. The pattern, adopted from one in Kenilworth England, called for a squat, almost square building, with arched French doors, between five and seven in number, on the sides, and two on the ends.

Situated halfway between Brockville and Toronto, Belleville was designated as a divisional point. But the station, as originally planned, was simply too small to handle all the staff needed for such a yard, and a separate building was added to house the administration and operations staff. As a result, the stone station was never needed as anything other than a waiting room.

Although it began as a single storey building, a second floor with a mansard roof was subsequently added, likely to accommodate community functions. Because no operator ever used the "station," the facade was never altered to add an operator's bay window as were most stations on the line. At some point, however, its full length French doors were filled part way to become windows.

Outside the station, the vast yards contained engine houses, repair sheds, and in 1910, received the largest roundhouse on the GT system, one which could accommodate 42 engines in stalls ninety feet (28m) deep. In the early years of the 20th century employment topped 1000 workers.

Beside the station were extensive gardens and lawns, while lining the street behind it were hotels and cafes to accommodate the needs of crew and passengers. Although the early streets of Belleville were laid out by the waterfront, the GT located its facilities, true to form, some distance inland. As a result, travellers needed to make their way some distance from town in order to ride the GT.

The cutbacks began in the 1950s with the conversion of engines from steam to diesel. Over the years which followed most of the divisional facilities were removed, including the repair shops, the office building, the freight station, and eventually, despite the protests of local residents, the large historic roundhouse. Within the station itself, many of the features were modernized and a separate stair tower added.

With the removal of so many nearby structures, the setting of the

Belleville station is now one of desert-like bleakness. The vast yards still extend in front of the station, which itself is surrounded by a large parking area. The string of stores and hotels still line the street, but are showing their age. While Belleville can justly boast a large number of preserved and designated heritage buildings, the station stands apart in an empty landscape.

It stands on Station Rd, south of the tracks and east of Cannifton Rd. It remains one of VIA Rail's busiest stations boasting 12 trains a day on the Toronto to Montreal and Ottawa corridor. In addition to the designation under the Station Act, the building has earned a National Historic Sites and Monuments Board plaque.

BRAMPTON
Like a Castle

As one approaches the Brampton station from the street, one might be forgiven for mistaking it for a small medieval castle. Above the entrance is a solid square castellated tower, while flanking it are two round towers with conical roofs. Of all the stations built by the Grand Trunk in Ontario, the one in Brampton is truly unique.

Before the GT began laying its route northwesterly from Toronto in the 1850s, Brampton was a small crossroads hamlet named Buffy's Corners, named for a roadside tavern owned by a resident of that name.

The towers on the Brampton station give it a decidedly castle-like appearance.

The first station built by the GT was a typical rural station suited to Brampton's small population, and followed the pattern of the Kenilworth style stations found with great frequency on the Montreal to Toronto portion. Other good examples still stand in Ernestown and at St Mary's Junction.

But as Brampton became the county seat and attracted more railways and businesses, the station quickly became obsolete. The turn of the century marked a major station building period for the GT, and a local councillor named John H. Boulter lobbied vigorously for a station with a distinctive style. While it is likely that Brampton was in line for a larger station anyway, Boulter's agitation brought about something special.

The original Brampton station was identical to the many pattern stations erected by the Grand Trunk.

That something was a brown brick chateau-style station, more typical of those being erected by the CPR, but unlike anything attempted by the GT to that time. The trackside was more traditional with a high Hanseatic gable dormer above the operator's bay, and a porte-cochere on the east end. Doors windows and pillars were all topped with rounded arches and the roof line was bellcast in form. The street side was dominated with three distinctive towers, all reminiscent of a medieval castle.

The GT did manage a few other stations of similar style, including the three wooden towers of the relocated Whitby Junction station, and the brick castle-like station which now serves as a library in downtown Petrolia.

Inside, the much renovated station consisted of the standard waiting room, ticket office and baggage area. While the baggage and express area are now closed and leased, the current ticket counter occupies roughly the same area as that used by the original operator.

Although the building is no great distance from Brampton's downtown, it does not visually link with it. It is surrounded by a parking lot and is generally not visible from the main downtown streets. All ancillary rail related buildings have been removed, although a number of early factory buildings still stand by the tracks west of the station.

The downtown area of Brampton is blessed with a wealth of heritage structures and the city's heritage supporters are working to save them, despite questionable decisions from a municipal council that is at times less than enthusiastic about its city's heritage. The GT station serves the railroading public with frequent GO Transit service and six daily VIA trains. It stands on Church Street west of Main.

BRANTFORD
Of Towers and Tiles

There is no mistaking the prominence of Brantford's Grand Trunk railway station. Its tall tower looms high above the surrounding buildings and the traffic which slips below the tracks on the West Street underpass. Its curved waiting room and steep tiled roof simply add to its elegance.

Yet if the Grand Trunk had brought its tracks to Brantford fifty years earlier, when it was first extending its route through southwestern Ontario, the city might have had to put up with a much more modest station.

Many of the historic interior features of the Brantford station still survive.

Although Brantford had its first railway line in 1854, the Buffalo and Brantford Railway was never a successful carrier. Its route angled from Fort Erie through Brantford and on to Goderich on Lake Huron. However, it was the lines built by the Grand Trunk and the Great Western from Toronto and Niagara Falls respectively to Sarnia and Windsor, with better access to the United States, which dominated. But Brantford was left off both. Instead, travellers from Brantford needed to follow a spur line to a junction with the GT's main line at Harrisburg, a route which was inconvenient and time consuming.

Finally, in 1905, as part of a major upgrading of the line's tracks and facilities, the GT re-routed its main line from Lynden through Brantford and back up to Paris. And in that year the city received a new station, one which was claimed to be "one of the most beautiful buildings in the city, but also one of the best depots on the entire Grand Trunk system."

That assessment is not too far off the mark. While its most prominent feature is its four storey tower, its two storey rounded waiting room is equally remarkable. Even the operator's bay window is surmounted with a conical roof while a gabled porte-cochere extends over the entrance. The building is constructed of bricks over a granite foundation and the roof is covered with red tile.

The waiting room was lined with tiled wainscotting to a height of two and half meters, topped with a leaf work border in gold and blue. Squared marble pillars extended to the ceiling where a brass chandelier with 20 incandescent lights was suspended with a heavy chain. The rounded bay window alcove served as the ladies waiting room. At the west end of the waiting room was the baggage room beside which were the ticket office and operator's bay where a switch board controlled the building's 141 electric lights. Unlike most stations of the day which were heated by stoves, that in Brantford could boast a modern steam-heated system.

While architectural enthusiasts may find such a style unusual in Ontario, it was decidedly not out of place in Michigan, for it was the

Detroit-based firm of Spier and Rohns which designed the building. It was this same firm which designed Grand Trunk stations throughout Michigan in Ann Arbour, Niles, Lansing, Grand Rapids and Battle Creek. All still stand, and most of them remain in railway use.

Surprisingly little has changed both in and around the Brantford station. The yards across from the station remain filled with freight cars, owned by RailLink. While a new ticket counter now fills in the former baggage room area, the tiled walls are still in place (although the chandelier has been replaced by a smaller fixture). Similarly, the brick and tile exterior, the tower and the varied roof line still make it one of Brantford's finest buildings. Indeed, the landscaped gardens beside the station recall the days when station agents competed with each other over who could grow the best garden.

While the arrival of the Grand Trunk main line in 1905 was too late to significantly affect Brantford's urban form, a number of railway related buildings still stand in the vicinity, including the former railway hotel on the east side of West Street. It still functions as a lounge.

But most important, passenger trains still call at the Brantford station. Eight VIA trains stop each day, six travelling between Toronto and Windsor, and two between Toronto and Sarnia.

A short distance east of Brantford lies the lovingly restored station at Caledonia. Although ineligible for federal designation, this 1905 Grand Trunk station was acquired by the local community, repainted into its original colours, and now operates as a museum. The tracks outside still echo to the wheels of a short line freight operation which serves the town's local industries.

Tiles and towers distinguish the majestic Brantford station.

CARTIER
The Station has the Groceries

Located in the northern woods more than 150 km from Sudbury, Cartier was an all railway town. When the CPR was ordered to build an all Canadian route, they surveyed their line northwestward from Sudbury. Divisional points were needed roughly at 150 km intervals which was as far as the steam engines could travel before needing a refill of coal. Here the engines would be serviced and crews would change shifts. Roundhouses, engine houses, and housing for employees were all integral parts of

The Cartier station in northern Ontario remains the focus of this former railway town.

the divisional town. In remote railway towns like Cartier, everything was brought in by train, even the groceries.

Prior to the arrival of the railway Cartier had been the site of a small logging community known as Slabtown. Although the CP wanted to name their station Archer, another town was using that name and the CP selected Cartier, after George-Etienne Cartier, a father of confederation.

The first station was a standard "Van Horne" style, a wooden barn-like structure two stories high. Because the CPR's railway builder, William Cornelius Van Horne had stipulated that the first stations be "the cheapest stations that can possibly be made," the CPR's first generation stations were identical in appearance, two stories high with simple end gables.

Within 15 years, the CPR began to flourish, and a new station philosophy dictated that stations be "as nearly perfect as possible without any regard to cost." As a result, the railway architects went to work preparing plans for larger and more attractive divisional stations. The Cartier station was built in 1910. The storey and a half storey structure now included wide gables at the ends and over the operator's bay. A cavernous waiting room occupied the east end of the building, a restaurant the west end, while the station manager's quarters took up the second floor.

In 1948 the building was significantly altered, doubling in size with a major addition to the west end. Ironically, this marked the approach of a period when railway divisional points were about to be drastically reduced.

The town too was built for and dependent upon the railway. Boarding houses, restaurants and family homes lined the grid network of streets north of the tracks. A YMCA was added and included a dance floor, gymnasium, bowling alley and dormitory rooms. The original station had been located on the north side of the yards, convenient to the town. The new station however was built south of the tracks, a location which meant that employees and passengers were forced to cross the extensive and busy yards. A petition for a pedestrian bridge was rejected by the railway.

Although a rough road was built from Sudbury in the 1930s, Cartier remained without a convenient highway connection until the 1960s. During this time the landscape around the station had been changing. The replacement of steam with diesel power for the engines meant the elimination of half the CP's divisional points. Staff numbers were reduced from more than 150 to fewer than a dozen. The Y was demolished in 1931, the other railway buildings a few decades later. The restaurant was eliminated and converted to offices and storage space.

Then the cuts to VIA in 1990 reduced passenger trains to the thrice weekly White River train.

The yards continue to hold rows of timber trains, while a much reduced CP crew continues to use the station building. Although the historic core of the town still lies north of the tracks, newer development has taken over along Highway 144 south of the tracks. The station is visible from Highway 144.

CASSELMAN
Small and Simple

To look at the simple style of the Casselman station would cause some to wonder at its selection as a "heritage" station. But the station was important to the community.

Casselman's single storey station is the third on the site and is typical of the buildings which the CN was constructing in the late 1930s. Its low hip roof with a small gable on each end contains none of the architectural ornaments which had embellished stations only a couple of decades earlier, no towers, no dormers, no grand waiting rooms. In fact Casselman station represented a utilitarian design concocted by CN's engineering department primarily for the line's western small town stations. It was adapted to only a few sites in eastern Canada (Atikokan and Jeannette's Creek were other examples).

The first station was built by the Canada Atlantic Railway in 1882. When it burned in 1899 a second station was built in its place. When fire struck again in 1938, the location for a third building was moved about 50 feet and a freight shed was erected on the foundation of the earlier station. A converted passenger coach served as a temporary station until the new one was finished.

Being in the heart of a prosperous farming area, the station typically shipped produce and even contained an egg candling facility. Otherwise, its interior design was as simple as its outside. A general waiting room was located at the west end, while the ladies' waiting area was located on the east, with the ticket office between. A baggage area was also located in the east section.

There were few other railway buildings around the station, however. While a lawn surrounded the board platform, a row of private homes lay close to the back of the station. A water tower stood some distance away near the site of the second station at Montcalm Street. But it burned in 1953 and was never replaced.

Although the location of the station had little impact on the way in which the town grew, the community had close ties to it. Many residents worked there, boarded the train for school there, or shipped off to war from its platform. Therefore, when the town was seeking an appropriate location for a museum, the station came immediately to the fore. However, the CN still needed the building and declined to part with it.

Today, passengers awaiting one of VIA Rail's three Montreal - Ottawa trains which call here each day use a shelter. As the community is only a half hour from Ottawa, many who travel from this point are commuters wisely avoiding the increasing traffic congestion around the city.

The wooden station, which remains in good condition, lies between St Isadore and Cartier Streets.

The simple station in Casselman now sees primarily commuter travel to Ottawa.

CHATHAM

The Tavern Was Too Noisy

A quick look at the Chatham railway station will reveal strong similarities between it and a handful of other grand stations in southern Ontario, namely those at Sarnia, Strathroy, Niagara Falls, and, to an extent, Woodstock. With their steep Gothic Revival rooflines and hip gables, all are either the work of, or have been influenced by, one of Ontario's most noteworthy station designers, Joseph Hobson.

As chief engineer and architect for first the Great Western Railway, and subsequently the Grand Trunk Railway, he also designed early stations at Hamilton and Windsor which no longer stand. Hobson started his career as a civil engineer on the early Grand Trunk during which time he designed the Suspension Bridge across the Niagara River. This led to his being hired as chief engineer for the Great Western Railway in 1873 where he designed not only a string of spectacular stations, but the tunnel under the St Clair River, considered an engineering marvel in its day.

The station which he provided for the booming riverside town of Chatham replaced an earlier building which had become too small, and sat in an undesirable location. Situated on the north side of the tracks beside a popular hotel, the early building was subject to noise and rowdyism from the busy tavern. Following local complaints, the GW placed the new building on the quieter south side of the tracks.

Hobson's bold new design featured three prominent gables placed on the steep roof, including a peak gable rising above the operator's bay in the centre, with a pair of hip gables prominently positioned over the ends of the building. Each gable represented a different function in the station below, the express and baggage functions in the end wings, the station master's offices in the middle, while the waiting rooms lay between. Although Chatham was not a railway divisional point; it was busy enough to support a dining room located in a separate building. In fact, the station and restaurant employed more than two dozen men and women.

A single storey flat-roofed freight shed extended from the west end of the station and was likely a later addition. All windows and doors displayed the pointed arches of the gothic style. The structure was brick with stonework used to highlight the main features. A prominent canopy extended around the entire building. Most of the interior features were modernized in the 1980s which resulted in the covering of most of the original woodwork, ceiling and trim. Proposals by VIA Rail to restore the building's heritage features were stalled when the federal government reduced its funding.

The distinctive roofline of Chatham's CN station is the trademark of one of Ontario's leading station architects, Joseph Hobson.

One problem with the station was its distance from the town. In the 1850s Chatham consisted only of a few mills and shipyards huddled on the banks of the Thames River. With the river navigable from this point to Lake St Clair, boats had been the chief mode of transportation up until this time. But when the railway line was built three km south of the river, businesses began to relocate there, among them the controversial tavern.

The Great Western Railway was built to provide an east-west short cut along which western American shippers could cross Ontario to reach the American seaboard. Later, when the rival Canada Southern Railway constructed a short cut of its own, line linking Fort Erie to Sarnia, the Great Western responded with yet a third line, the Canada Air Line, parallel to the CS. When the CPR began its intrusion into southwestern Ontario, its main rival, the Grand Trunk, quickly gobbled up most of the local lines, including the Great Western.

Following the Great Western, two other railway lines entered Chatham, the Erie and Huron providing a north-south link between Sarnia and Erieau on Lake Erie, and the Canadian Pacific with another east-west line directly through the centre of the town. The CPR station was a solid brick building with a wide arch marking the entrance. It now sits in a garden centre east of town. The EH, which is now part of the CSX system, still uses a small brick station on Colborne Street at the east end of the city.

Chatham remains a busy railway town. Although freight trains call much less frequently now, VIA trains still call at the Chatham station eight times a day. The building is situated on Queen Street a little north of Park Avenue which leads from the 401 as County Road 40. And across the tracks from the station, stands a small railway museum, as well as the once notorious hotel which still functions as a tavern.

COBOURG
A True Small Town Station

Among the many heritage stations still standing in small town Ontario, that in Cobourg is the most lively, and adheres most truly to the station tradition. The waiting room has been restored to its early appearance and is often filled with passengers awaiting one of VIA Rail's frequent trains, while a café offers light meals, and hosts community meetings.

From the earliest days of settlement in central Ontario, Cobourg has been a key transportation hub. Its deep harbour on Lake Ontario ensured its effectiveness as a port from which people and products could arrive and depart. This facility was instrumental in its obtain-

The attractive station in Cobourg is one of Ontario's busiest.

ing the rights to build the area's first railway to the hinterland, the Cobourg Peterborough and Chemong Railway in 1854. However, the perilous crossing over Rice Lake doomed the line and the crossing was eliminated in 1860.

In 1856 the Grand Trunk added its own rails, located, as was that railway's custom, well away from the water so as to not benefit its competing lake shippers. The GT's first facilities included a long low wooden station, an agent's house, maintenance shops and a restaurant, all inconveniently situated on the north side of the tracks, while the town lay on the south side.

After the reduction of the Cobourg and Peterborough Railway, Cobourg's main rival, Port Hope, extended its own line to the hinterland, the Port Hope Lindsay and Beaverton Railway (which later became part of the extensive Midland Railway system), and Cobourg's own growth stagnated. But it become an attractive haven for American tourists, in particular wealthy iron manufacturers from Pittsburgh who had become familiar with the town through its connection to the Marmora iron mines further north.

Soon these summer families began building grand summer homes. Then, as part of its upgrading in the 1890s, and to tie into the burgeoning tourism market, the GT decided to replace the station at Cobourg.

In 1911 GT architect L.M. Watts took a set of station plans which J.M. Bearbrook had prepared for the Guelph station some years before, and modified them for the Cobourg station. About this time a new rival railway, the Canadian Northern Railway, presented to the Board of Railway Commissioners plans for a station it too wanted to build in Cobourg. The Board sensibly insisted that the companies build a joint station. However, the GT resisted, and Cobourg came to have two stations within meters of each other. A third was also added nearby when the Canadian Pacific Railway added its own line in 1912.

Located more logically on the south side of the tracks, the new station was an appealing structure. It was constructed of brick upon a stone foundation and measured 27' by 150' (10m by 50m). Its style was categorized as Romanesque Revival. The large central waiting room was flanked by separate facilities for ladies and gents. The west wing housed a restaurant while the east wing contained the express and baggage facilities. The waiting room was attractively paneled with ornate wainscotting topped by arches.

In 1994 VIA Rail invested a quarter of a million dollars in restoring the heritage of the building. The drop ceilings of the CN era were torn out, and the woodworking of the ceiling and the walls was restored. Bricks, roof and soffit and fascia were all upgraded. The ticket counter was removed from the bay to the site of the former restaurant, while a café was installed in the former baggage area. Plastic seats were replaced by more authentic wooden benches.

Although a few freight cars still park on the sidings, the area around the station has changed. A large parking lot for daily commuters now extends well to the west while the CP and Canadian Northern stations have both long disappeared from the landscape. (The Canadian Northern had abandoned its entire line by 1940.)

Still, the station is one of the most pleasant to visit. For train watchers, ten passenger trains call here each day, while the CP main line behind offers frequent freight trains. And between trains, there is the café and gift shop to visit. Cobourg's historic core lies about a km to the south. Close by, the harbour has been renovated to accommodate tourists. Sadly, most of the grand homes built by the Americans a century ago have gone.

The station is located on the west side of Division Street three blocks north of University Avenue.

BRIGHTON

Although not designated under the HRSPA, the station at Brighton, just four station stops east of Cobourg, has been preserved as a local heritage site thanks largely to the efforts of just one man.

The last surviving GT station of the Kenilworth plan to have been built of brick (others were Grafton and Colborne) the building saw its last passenger train in 1964 and had it not served as a communications center for the CN, would have been demolished soon after. One of three stations to have served the town, it was the first, and the only station for nearly fifty years until the Canadian Northern and the CPR built lines and stations within a few meters of each other.

Although much altered on the outside, four of the ten arched French doors were replaced with maintenance shed doors, the operator's office retained much of its woodwork. For the most part however the building was in a deteriorating condition. And that is how Ralph Bangay found it when he purchased it from the CNR for $25,000 in 1996. Although his original intent was to simply store the Brighton memorabilia he had accumulated over the years, the station took on a life of its own. Bangay gradually added railway items to his collection and the station is now known across North America as Memory Junction museum.

Bangay and his volunteers have also rescued a considerable amount of railway rolling stock, including a caboose, boxcar, boarding car, and a steam engine which for years had sat unattended and vandalized in a Belleville park. Although the train doesn't stop here any more, Memory Junction provides ample train watching as it sits on the busiest sections of both the CN and CPR main lines from Toronto to Montreal and Ottawa.

It is located at the foot of Maplewood, formerly Railroad St, in Brighton.

Memory Junction reflects the work of one individual to save the Brighton station from demolition.

COCHRANE
The Station is Growing

The two storey brick station in the northern community of Cochrane is one of a kind. It can claim to be the only such structure to contain a hotel in its second storey.

The station in Cochrane began as a "union" station, or one which is shared by two or more railway companies. After the Ontario government had completed its Temiskaming and Northern Ontario Railway line to New Liskeard in 1903, the federal government of Wilfrid Laurier unveiled plans for a new cross country route, the National Transcontinental Railway, to be built from Quebec City in

The roof of the Cochrane station has been radically altered since this early view, and many of the decorative features have been removed.

the east to Prince Rupert in the west. Upon hearing of that decision, the TNO quickly decided to extend its tracks northward to meet those of the new line. The junction would be at a location later to be called Cochrane.

The TNO surveyors got there first, choosing a site around a series of small lakes for the terminus and a new town. The water from the lakes would be crucial for both the town residents and rail operations. Also, by being first, the TNO could enjoy watching the NTR construct and pay for the crossing between the two lines.

Not only would the location be a terminus for the TNO but also a divisional point for the NTR. The TNO commissioned their architect, John M. Lyle to design the station. Two stories high, the building was ornamented with a cupola and cross gables, with attractive dormers on both north and south sides. Inside was a sizable restaurant and a two storey waiting room.

While the TNO yards sprawled to the south of the station, the tracks of the NTR passed on the north. Both railways added roundhouses, repair shops, water towers, and bunkhouses.

The town itself was laid out north of the station in a grid pattern of streets, a plan typical of railway towns. When the lots went up for auction, they quickly sold out at $300 each. However, to discourage speculation, purchasers were required to build a structure on the lot within a year. By 1914, trains were running on the NTR, six years after service on the TNO portion began. When forest fires ravaged the town in 1910, 1911 and again in 1916, the brick station protected the residents while most other buildings burned. Relief for the fire victims was brought in by train.

In 1930 the TNO decided on even further expansion and extended their own line north to the Arctic tidewater at Moosonee. Its plans for an ocean port, however, were thwarted by the unpredictable shifting sand bars at the mouth of the Moose River, and the new terminus became instead a supply point for the Cree communities along the James Bay coast. Later, as tourists began to discover this frontier corner of the province, the Ontario Northland (as the TNO was renamed after World War II) began its popular Polar Bear Express, a summer-time excursion train.

But despite the boom in tourism, rail operations in Cochrane were declining. With the conversion to diesel, the CN, which had assumed the NTR in 1923, no longer needed a divisional point here and demolished most of its divisional structures, its staff plunging from 200 to ten. Although the ONR likewise switched to diesel, the railway retained Cochrane as an important terminal point for both passenger and freight service.

During the 1960s, the station changed too. Nearly all of the roof ornamentations, the cupola, and the gables were removed in favour of a shallower and simpler roof line.

Despite the popularity of the Polar Bear Express, regular passenger service through Cochrane was steadily cut back. Cuts by the federal government of Brian Mulroney in 1990 eliminated VIA service between Cochrane and Kapuskasing, and Cochrane and Toronto. In 1997 the Ontario government halved ONR service between

The train from Cochrane to Senneterre Quebec has been discontinued.

Cochrane and Toronto, and, as of this writing, is considering putting the operation out to bid. The last of the passenger services on the old NTR ended in 1998 when VIA canceled its weekly run from Cochrane to Senneterre. (Trains still operate from Senneterre to Montreal, a run that is packed with regular cottagers and campers, and presents an eye-opening experience for visitors as well.)

In the early 1990s, the building was once again altered, this time to enhance its services to passengers. Gables were restored to the roof, the waiting area was enlarged (although a drop ceiling unfortunately has covered the high ceiling) and hotel rooms were added to the second floor. A new two storey building, of compatible design, was added to the west of the station and now contains a modern restaurant.

Ontarians are discovering northeastern Ontario, and over the past two decades Cochrane has enjoyed a boom in tourism. Motels now line Highway 11 and are often fully booked during the summer with Polar Bear Express excursionists. Yet the town, with its unusually wide main street and grid of residential streets still looks and behaves very much like the railway town it still is.

Cochrane lies 750 km north of Toronto on Highway 11.

COBALT

Between Cochrane and North Bay, the Temiskaming and Northern Ontario Railway erected a string of identical stations. Their standard plan was for a storey-and-a-half wooden structure with a bell cast roof and a hip dormer puncturing the roofline. All have since been replaced, demolished, or burned in one of the northland's many devastating forest fires.

The station at Cobalt lasted for a mere five years. While scouting for timber suitable for railway ties, a pair of timber scouts happened upon a boulder containing rich silver ore. A standard station was built at the location and given the name Cobalt, after the parent ore which normally contains the silver. But as the silver boom swept the region, the station proved to be inadequate, and architect John Lyle,

Silver waits like loaves of bread for shipment from the Cobalt station during the height of the silver boom.

who had designed the station at Cochrane and later helped design Toronto's union station, was commissioned to design a station more fitting to a boom town.

In 1909 the building was opened. Built of brick, it was dominated by a two storey central section, with a ladies' waiting room, a ticket and telegraph office on the main floor, and more offices upstairs. At the north end the general waiting room, with its 18-foot ceiling, was lit by dormer windows in the roof, while the south end was dedicated to baggage.

Its exterior design consisted of a semi-circular arched dormer above the second floor window, with two dormers on each side of the waiting room, and a fifth dormer at the end. A covered porte-cochere extended over the platform at the south end. The building stretched for 148' (50m) along the track.

Built on almost impossible rocky ridges, the town stretched out above the building, with the main street and its half mile of stores dominating a ridge beside the tracks. At its peak Cobalt boomed to a population of 10,000 and was the centre of more than 200 mines, many right in the town itself.

By the 1930s the boom had fizzled out. Mines were closed and the population plunged to fewer than 2,000. By 1985, most of the main street had fallen victim to a series of fires and the station was closed. Although it could not be federally designated (being owned by a provincially chartered railway) the station was nonetheless considered to be a key heritage building for the community which commissioned a feasibility study for its re-use. A decade later it was opened as a privately- run military museum. Because the ONR is a provincially-chartered railway, stations which it owns are not eligible for designation under a Federal act.

Cobalt, with its boomtown landscape, is one of Ontario's most historic towns, and the station remains one of its most important silver boom buildings.

Cobalt lies east of Highway 11, about 140 km north of North Bay. The station is on the main street.

TEMAGAMI

Although much smaller than the station at Cobalt, that at Temagami more than makes up for it in sheer visual appeal. It too replaced an earlier standard style and was opened in 1909. The original building served as a restaurant for a number of years after that. A decorative flower garden stretched out to the north of the building.

By this time, the TNO was starting to diversify its operations and began to target the tourist trade. Tourists were beginning to discover the beauty of Lake Temagami's old growth forests. From a dock near the station steamers plied the waters of the lake. To enhance its appeal to those arriving to board the steamers, the TNO decided a new station was in order.

The striking new building was built of stone. A pronounced gable rose above the central portion, embellished with a Tudor revival trim which extended down to include both the operator's bay window on the track side, and a decorative bay window on the street side. Inside a cathedral ceiling gave the two waiting rooms, ladies' to the south, gents' to the north, the appearance of a grand hall.

Unsympathetic renovations over the years covered the high ceilings and much of the interior woodwork. Today, the station is in the hands of the Temagami Station Restoration Trust, which is restoring the building to much of its early appearance, as well as preparing for the inclusion of a small museum and commercial operation. Little else of historic note has managed to survive in this roadside town. Happily, the station still visually dominates the townscape, a lonely legacy of the town's railway heritage. Again, as an ONR station, it is not federally designated.

Temagami straddles Highway 11 about 100 km north of North Bay.

The beautiful stone station in the former resort town of Temagami is being restored by a local development trust.

COMBER
The Last Original Station

It may seem odd indeed that such a simple station as the one in Comber would successfully receive federal heritage designation, while a more elaborate and attractive building, such as that designed by Joseph Hobson in Strathroy, would be rejected. Yet it was just such simplicity which earned the little building its status.

The Canada Southern Railway was built from Fort Erie to Windsor and Sarnia to provide American shippers with a short cut across

The simple style of the Comber station marks it as an original.

The station at Comber was never a busy spot.

Ontario. Although some of its structures, such as the elongated station in St Thomas, were architecturally outstanding, most of the railway's original stations were built to as simple a pattern as possible. That at Comber is the sole survivor of this breed. Small in scale, the building is rectangular with a wide shallow pitched roof and gables at each end. The original siding was board and batten. The interior of the station was equally simple with a waiting room at one end, baggage and express facilities at the other, and the operator's and agent's office between.

Prior to the arrival of the railway in 1873, Comber was little more than a rural hamlet. The arrival of the station attracted four hotels, feed mills, lumber mills and other rural industries to rail side. Soon a new community was flourishing around the tracks. Comber was also the junction of a branch line to the Lake Erie resort of Seacliffe, now a part of Leamington. With the recent conversion of Leamington's ketchup factory from rail to truck, the branch line is no longer used.

Major highway construction in the 1930s began to draw travellers from the trains and into cars and buses, and by 1941 passenger service at Comber was discontinued. CN revamped the interior of the building in 1970 to accommodate its own crews and then later covered over the distinctive board and batten exterior with aluminum siding.

Today, most of the trackside industries are gone, and only a single hotel lingers on the main street, now converted to a residence.

Many little villages which grew around stations, not only along the Canada Southern, but on the now-abandoned Canada Air Line Railway further south, still survive, although many now are beginning to resemble the weathered ghost towns more typical of the railway lines in Saskatchewan.

ESSEX

Most other stations in the area have been demolished, or burned. However, restored stone stations can be found in Kingsville and Essex, both to the southwest of Comber.

Now preserved, the stone station in Essex reflects an American architectural style.

Unlike the station at Comber, that in Essex is not original. In 1887, as part of its upgrading policy, the Michigan Central Railway, which was leasing the Canada Southern, built one of the finest small town stone stations in Ontario. Using the influence of H.H. Richardson, America's most prolific station architect of the era, the building was typically squat with a wide arch around the waiting room door. A low tower covered a porte-cochere at the street side entrance.

The general waiting room ceiling extended the full storey and a half roof, and was extra lit by a three windowed dormer. Both waiting rooms, including the one reserved for ladies on the opposite end of the building, were finely paneled. The building was constructed of Saginaw field stone with split faces and trimmed with stone from the Credit Valley.

Then on August 10, 1907, it seemed that the lovely station would meet a premature end. That night a boxcar containing 5,000 pounds of explosives blew apart, killing two railway workers and causing extensive damage to several buildings. However, the heavy stone wall of the station stood firm, and the damage to it was repaired.

The station is now owned by the town of Essex, and at one time housed a gift shop and art gallery. Future plans include a museum and archives. Essex is situated on Highway 3, southeast of Windsor and the station can be found at the corner of Station and Fox Sts.

ERNESTOWN
A Rural Vestige

Most of Ontario's federally designated heritage railway stations lie in cities or towns. The little stone station at the hamlet of Ernestown is their sole surviving country cousin.

In order to avoid exorbitant prices demanded by landowners at what was originally Ernest Town, now Bath, the Grand Trunk Railway, in 1856, laid its tracks well inland. In fact its "Ernestown" station ended up being more than 6 km from Bath. The closest settlement of any description at the time was a collection of mills on Mill Creek known as Links Mills.

Ernestown's country station was seldom a busy place.

Because of its remoteness, a small satellite village grew around the station consisting of a few homes, as well as an agent's house, freight platform and barn by the station. The rural flag stop saw few passengers, and trains stopped mainly to pick up the mail and the milk. Typical of the standard station plans of the GTR, the station at Ernestown had rows of French doors along the sides and ends, a low shallow roof and four corner chimneys. Being a smaller variation of this plan, Ernestown had only five French doors while the largest example, at Prescott, had seven. Inside, the station was divided into the usual passenger, operational and baggage sections.

Because of its low level of passenger use, little about the station has changed. While the French doors were filled in to create windows, no operator's bay window was ever added. As a result the station retains the same overall appearance as when it was first built in 1855. Although the exterior of the station is little altered, much of the inside was divided up to provide rooms for railway maintenance crews.

Passenger trains stopped calling altogether in the 1950s, and freight trains not long after that. The building continued to be used by maintenance crews until the 1990s. By then all ancillary railway buildings had been removed, and most of the original dwellings in the hamlet of Ernestown have been replaced now by modern homes.

Urban sprawl has not yet overwhelmed the landscape in this part of the country and the fields and woodlots which surround the lonely building have helped retain the flavour of a purely country station found nowhere else in Ontario. Here, on the busy Montreal to Toronto main line of the CN, both passenger and freight trains rumble past at frequent intervals. But the little stone station can only sit and watch.

Ernestown lies on County Road 4, 8 km south of Highway 401 and about 20 km west of Kingston.

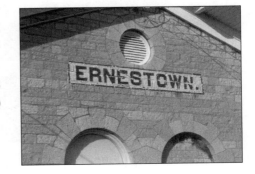

The hand-painted sign still survives on the Ernestown station.

FORT FRANCES
It's a Long Storey

The dominant impression of Fort Frances' historic Canadian Northern station is its unusual length. Because its central portion was designed in the style of the Canadian Northern's country stations, and measured only 32 by 24 feet (10m by 7m), its many additional facilities needed to be housed in single storey extensions on either side which measured in total 180 feet (55m).

When the Canadian Northern Railway opened the line in 1901-2, it connected Winnipeg with Port Arthur and marked the beginning

The station in Fort Frances is an unusually long structure.

of an ambitious new transcontinental railway line. The enterprising railway building duo of William MacKenzie and Donald Mann began their empire by acquiring a defunct short line railway charter in southern Manitoba in 1899. By adding to it unused charters and undervalued short lines, the two were, by 1913, able to open what was then Canada's second cross-country railway. And Fort Frances was right on that line.

The first Fort Frances station was a two storey wooden building with a tower on one of the trackside corners. But with the opening in 1912 of an extension across the international border to Duluth Minnesota, the old station proved inadequate.

In 1913 the Winnipeg office of the CNOR adapted an R.B Pratt design for the new station. While the main portion, with its trademark two-storey pyramid roof resembled the many country stations which the railway had constructed, its two extensive wings housed the extra divisional and customs facilities required in this location. The west end of the station housed customs, immigration and detention rooms, all of which had to be isolated from the rest of the building. Next came a bonded storage area and baggage room. In the centre were the waiting rooms and station agent's facilities. The east extension, which was added in 1928, housed the express rooms and additional offices. The entire building is constructed of red brick and rests on a concrete foundation.

The original station was relocated to the east of the new building and served as dispatch offices and a restaurant. Out in the extensive divisional yards were a five-stall roundhouse, engine house, coal dock, water tower, freight shed and the usual tool houses and storage sheds. Laid out in a grid pattern, Fort Frances was typical of the many divisional railway towns across northern Ontario.

With the arrival of diesel power in the 1960s, the facility was downgraded and most of the divisional buildings removed. The restaurant housed in the original station burned in 1967.

For most of its existence, the town of Fort Frances could only be reached by train. That era ended in 1965 with the opening of a new

The original Fort Frances station still stood to the left of its newer, larger replacement, and was serving as a restaurant when this photo was snapped.

highway to Fort William and Port Arthur. A decade later passenger service ended and CN closed the station a few years after that, threatening to demolish it. Following a decision by the town council to not fund the purchase of the vacant station the local citizens rallied to save the building and today it houses the Fort Frances Volunteer Bureau.

Fort Frances has grown beyond its railway days. The new highway brought with it motels and restaurants and its main industry today is the pulp mill which dominates the townscape.

The station is located at 140 Fourth Street West.

RAINY RIVER

Because it had been purchased by the town of Rainy River prior to the enactment of the HRSPA, the stunning brick station in the centre of town did not require federal designation. Built in 1913, the Rainy River station was not typical of that railway's stations. It lacked the usual pyramid roof and has instead a prominent gable over the centre of the building on both the track and street sides.

Like Fort Frances, Rainy River was a divisional town and a border point, for it is here that the railway crosses the Rainy River and enters the United States at Baudette Minnesota before reentering Canada at Manitoba.

The tiny town of Rainy River resembles in its appearance a typical prairie railway town with a wide main street of single storey stores ending at the station's back door. Indeed, all of Rainy River country, with its flat black soils and railway towns, is much like a piece of the prairies which somehow became stranded in Ontario.

Although the train crews still end their shifts here, they do so in newer facilities. The yards now stand empty and CN declared the station redundant. During the 1980s, the town assembled funds with the help of the Ontario Ministry of Municipal Affair's PRIDE program and purchased the building for community use. Although the trains don't stop here anymore, the former station remains, as it did in its railway days, the most prominent building in town.

The pretty station in this prairie-like town is now a community facility.

GALT
A Case of Neglect

By the time the Canadian Pacific Railway came to Galt and built its station high on a hill above the Grand River, Galt was already a bustling and prosperous town. Thanks to the swiftly flowing waters of the river, Galt had by 1830 acquired several mills. Although the Great Western Railway had extended a branch into town from its main line at Harrisburg in 1855, the town was anxious for still more railway connections, and in 1873 offered the Credit Valley Railway a bonus of $110,000 to build through it.

Maintenance has slipped on the CPR's historic Galt station.

Over the next two decades more lines followed including the electrified Galt Preston and Hespeler Railway, the Grand River Railway and the Lake Erie and Northern. A branch of the Grand Trunk was extended down the west side of the river where its small stone station still stands, now minus its tracks.

By 1898 the Credit Valley Railway had been incorporated into the CPR's vast system, a year which saw the start of major upgrades both to tracks and structures. To design its more important Ontario stations, the CPR hired a Canadian architect named Edward Maxwell, reversing a practice of hiring exclusively American firms. Nonetheless, Maxwell had worked in the U.S and was schooled in what is known as the Richardsonian Romanesque style of architecture, a style which is typified by wide arches and low squat massings, and used extensively in the eastern United States.

In 1898 Maxwell imported the new trend into Canada applying it at stations in Moose Jaw, Vancouver, and Ottawa. Its most elaborate manifestation was at the magnificent chateauesque station/hotel in McAdam, New Brunswick. In Ontario, Maxwell created similar stations at Woodstock (extant), Chatham (relocated) and Guelph (dismantled).

Opened in 1899, the Galt station was built of brick on a stone foundation. Although it rose only a single storey, it was spacious enough to contain the offices required to run a divisional yard. The street side entrance was highlighted with a broad gable above a recessed porch and a four-panelled wood door topped with an arched transom. A wide overhang surrounded the building, giving shelter on all sides. An eyebrow dormer, since removed, sat above the bay on the track side with the words "CPR Galt" painted inside the rounded gable.

Inside the station, the large waiting room took up the western end of the building, while the agent's office and other railway functions filled the eastern section. A separate, less elaborate, baggage building was added on the east. In its heyday, 22 trains would call each day to carry passengers west to Chatham, London or Windsor, or east to

Guelph Junction and North Toronto.

Sadly, under the CPR's indifferent care, the building has lost most of its detailing. The windows and wainscotting inside are lost amid drop ceilings, plywood panelling and linoleum floors. Around the building, a potholed parking area has replaced the once extensive gardens. As Parks Canada's designation report laments, the "once lovely station has suffered the depredations of expedient repair and explicit neglect."

Other than related railway buildings, the station had little impact on surrounding development. The coaling docks, water towers and stock yards have all disappeared from the landscape.

CPR has recently launched a funding program to support local heritage projects which have links to the CPR. One might hope that the CPR's heightened interest in its own heritage might eventually translate into the restoration of some of its own stations as well. If so, the station in Galt would be a good start.

Galt's CPR station lies on Malcolm Street, just east of Water Street North. Immediately to the west, the massive railway bridge spans the Grand River. Several other heritage buildings can be found along the river in the core area of the town, and include the old town hall, the market, and 19th century mills.

GEORGETOWN
The Urbanization of a Station

Just to look at the Grand Trunk station in Georgetown Ontario, is to tell that it is a hybrid. Not just a mix of station styles, it also represents an amalgam of station eras.

It was built in 1858 in the Grand Trunk's usual style for its stone stations, that is wide and squat with a low roof line and arched French doors lining the sides. When the Hamilton and Northwestern Railway came through town linking Lake Erie with Georgian Bay, it added its own station a little to the west of that of the Grand Trunk.

The enlargement of the Georgetown station is evident on its end wall.

After the latter line absorbed its smaller rival it unveiled a proposal for a union station where the two lines met. But the financial downturn of the 1890s killed that plan. Instead the GT opted to revitalize the original building.

By this time, towers and turrets had become the rage in the United States, and were part of a trend that was making an impact upon Canadian station design as well. As a result, the GT decided to totally revamp the Georgetown station with a much steeper roof and a pair of eight-sided towers on its two track side corners. It was a prosperous period for the railway company as it upgraded no fewer than 60 stations and built for itself a new headquarters in Montreal as well.

Georgetown had begun as a mill town on the Credit River, much of it centred on the woolen mill and foundry established by the Barber Brothers in 1831. When the Grand Trunk built through the area, as was its practice, it avoided the higher priced lands of the town's built-up area. When the HNW came through 2 decades later, the town had already become a bustling retail and industrial centre.

With many of the early railway functions now gone, along with most of the early industries, Georgetown's role has changed yet again. Engulfed by the urban sprawl that is spilling across the Greater Toronto Area, it has become a bedroom community, supplying commuters for the area's major cities. As a result, GO Transit rail service was extended to Georgetown in 1974, and the station was upgraded to accommodate the increased use.

The interior is now entirely devoted to a waiting room, with separate ticket counters for GO and VIA Rail passengers. The drop ceiling was removed to reveal the height of the original ceiling, while the wall designs recreate the atmosphere of an earlier railway era. Most of the improvements were undertaken by VIA. An additional building provided by GO Transit is not compatible with the station and detracts from the station's otherwise historic ambience.

The station's end gables, now higher and steeper, reveal the outline of the older and lower roof line that marked the original station. As with most of the Grand Trunk's early stone stations, the five arched French doors of the original design were filled in to create windows, with one covered over entirely to allow for an operator's bay window.

Outside, a large parking lot now surrounds the building, and an extensive yard for GO trains occupies the former sorting yard. Of the other early buildings, only the old railway hotel still stands across the track. Although five VIA trains call most days, including the VIA/Amtrak Chicago trains, most traffic is generated by GO Transit.

The station is located north of King Street and west of Mountainview Road.

Despite the milk cans in this early view, Georgetown station today primarily moves commuters.

GUELPH
Towering Over the Town

It is somehow fitting that one of Ontario's most heritage-conscious cities would be visually so dominated by its two most important historic buildings, the city hall and the Grand Trunk railway station.

Guelph was a city that had to fight for its railway, and the station

that it has today. In order to encourage a railway line through Guelph, the city acquired an earlier railway charter, since abandoned by its owners, and in 1851-2 built its own line to Toronto. This initiative encouraged the GTR to include Guelph on its proposed Toronto to Chicago route. By 1856 the GT had completed the line through Guelph, and built a station in the downtown area beside the market square.

The first depot followed the railway's standard pattern of a square low building with a

The Guelph station might never have had its tower had it not been for local lobbying.

shallow pitched roof, and rows of French windows, similar to that still standing at St Mary's Junction. In fact, several were built to this design on the Sarnia branch including the original stations at Brampton and Stratford, both of which were later replaced.

In the years which followed, Guelph attracted wealthy immigrants from the U.K., many coming because of the railway connection. By 1875 the city had over 8500 inhabitants. With the rapid increase in both freight and passenger movement, the station soon became inadequate.

Local citizens and politicians lobbied doggedly for a new station, not only one that was larger, but one which suited the town's stature. And so began the story of the tower that grew. The first station design, prepared by J.M. Bearbrook, was a low simple structure, with a gable above the street side porte-cochere. But with the rising popularity of dominant station towers, especially on the Grand Trunk stations in the United States, the citizenry demanded a tower on theirs as well. In 1907 a small tower, of roof height, was incorporated into the plans.

But by the time the station was completed in 1911 the tower had grown considerably and when finally constructed, was higher than the more modest early version. Unfortunately, the location of the new building was right in the middle of the town's market square, an area set aside by its original designers, John Galt, to give the town a distinctive urban form. But with the new station, the square was gone.

Immediately west of the station rose the attractive town hall, and from their positions on either side of Wellington St, the main commercial core, the two buildings visually dominated the town. Many new commercial buildings were added in this period as well, several built of stone.

But the station drew the most admiration. Constructed of grey granite and buff brick, and roofed with green tile, it stood at the head of a circular drive which passed through the garden area. The main waiting room opened into a grand hall which boasted a high ceiling and wainscotting trimmed with quarter cut oak. A main feature was the ornate five-sided ticket booth located directly across from the main entrance. In addition to the main waiting room were a ladies' parlour and a men's smoking room.

Changes to the station and its environs have not been sympathetic to its original design. These have included replacing the garden with a parking lot (although a small garden area remains), covering the waiting room wall with gyproc, and changing the positioning of the ticketing counters. The exterior happily has undergone few changes, with the exception of replacing the roof tiles with asbestos shingles. Unlike those stations in Stratford and Kitchener, which lost their towers to renovations, that on the Guelph station still soars high above the street.

Thanks to the concerted effort of Guelph's citizens, and many of its politicians, much remains of Guelph's built heritage. And the towered station is one of those successes.

VIA Rail has recently added a new train to the Kitchener Toronto corridor and Guelph now enjoys six daily trains during the week, including the jointly run Amtrak/VIA train to Chicago.

A track-side view of the Guelph station.

HAMILTON CN
The Last of the Classics

The trains will never again stop at Hamilton's remarkable CN railway station. Below the waiting room and the concourse, VIA and Amtrak passenger trains glide noise-lessly past, a contrast to the rumbling of the occasional freight trains. Yet, despite the loss of the railways, this architecturally acclaimed building has again become a key community gathering point.

The legacy of Hamilton's "CN" station dates back to 1853 with the arrival of the Great Western Railway. Here, beneath the gaze of his Dundurn Castle, Allan McNab, the railway's president, located not just their station, but their yards, shops and headquarters. The first station followed the GW's first generation pattern of long low wooden buildings with little in the way of archi-tectural finery. But its situation beside the harbour meant that as traffic rapidly increased, it

The grand foyer of the Hamilton CN station has been restored.

soon became obsolete. In 1875, following several additions, the station was replaced by a handsome new brick building, similar in design to today's Niagara Falls station.

Then a string of dramatic changes affected the fate of the station. In 1882, the Grand Trunk, which up until then had been the GW's main rival, assumed the GW's assets and six years later relocated the headquarters. Then, in 1895, a rival came to town in the form of the newly built Toronto Hamilton and Buffalo Railway. The newcomer's station, a beautiful brick building, was much more convenient to Hamilton's flourishing downtown than was the distant GT station.

But it was not until after the CN took over the then bankrupt GT in 1923 that the new president, Henry Thornton, decided to relocate the station. Here, on Hamilton's main north-south artery, James St, Thornton ordered CN's architect, John Schofield, to design one of his trademark classical stations. It was opened in 1931.

The grounds of the Hamilton CN station have been newly landscaped.

Originally the station was to be part of a proposed "City Beautiful" movement, a scheme which envisioned an amphitheater, a union station, and a wide tree-lined avenue to connect the two. But the proposal sputtered, and the only evidence of the grand plan was a large lawn in front of the new station building.

Hamilton's CN station is visually reminiscent of Toronto's wonderful Union Station opened just four years earlier. Two storey pillars mark the oversized entrance, between them are friezes of railway scenes. The waiting room, however, held travellers in awe. Two stories high, the room featured three ceiling panels, with blue and gold ornamentation. From the ceiling hung two massive bronze lanterns. From the waiting room a wide concourse led to the stairs which descended to tracks below.

By 1990, however, CN and VIA had both moved out, and GO trains stopped calling two years later. Ignored, the building began to deteriorate. Then in 1996, Hollywood saved the day. To help prepare the building for the movie, *The Long Kiss Goodnight*, starring Geena Davis, the movie makers spent more than $1 million making essential repairs. The building's future was further reaffirmed when Parks Canada declared it a National Heritage Railway Station.

Finally, in 1998, the Labourer's International Union of North America (LIUNA) bought the property and converted it to an office building and banquet facility. While the concourse has been extensively altered, the waiting room has been carefully restored, and the wide lawn in front landscaped into a public garden. While the interior is generally limited to users of the facility, the grounds and the facade offer ample opportunity to enjoy the beauty of Schofield's work. There is ample free parking.

The building is located on James Street at the corner of Murray Street.

Train spotters can enjoy the rail traffic from the sidewalk which crosses the bridge, including the mid-morning and late afternoon Amtrak passenger train, the New York-bound *Maple Leaf*. VIA trains to and from Niagara Falls pass in the early morning and late afternoon.

A short distance west of the station is the historic railway customs house, now a municipal building, while a short distance west of that is the access to Hamilton's new waterfront park. It is conveniently situated beside the freight yards, and the site of Hamilton's first station, where train spotters can watch the action of the short line "RailLink" company.

Amtrak's *Maple Leaf* slips past the platforms of the Hamilton CN station before they were removed.

HAMILTON, THB
The Art Deco Invasion

The legacy of railway stations in Hamilton is truly a tale of two stations. Both built at roughly the same time, one exhibits the traditional classical lines of an era of station building which was drawing to a close, while the other proclaimed the bold sleek lines of a new age in architecture. The latter was that built by the Toronto Hamilton And Buffalo Railway.

By 1890 southern Ontario was crisscrossed by a dense network of railway lines, leaving few areas unserviced. However, the pro-

Hamilton's THB station was the only large station in Ontario to display the art deco style of architecture

moters of the Toronto Hamilton and Buffalo saw an opportunity to link the booming industrial city at the head of the lake with the lucrative American markets by building a connection to such existing lines as the Canada Southern and the Michigan Central. In 1895 the first train headed west from the lavish new station at Hunter and James Sts, to the small town of Waterford located on the Michigan Central line.

The first station was a classical Victorian station constructed of stone and sporting a tower on one corner. While older lines were failing due to over-building or were victims of the depression, the THB wisely added a loop line through the wall of steel plants which lined the lake to the north. Not only did the THB thus survive the depression, but it was ready to build a new station.

When the CN indicated that it was ready to add a new station of its own, pressure was exerted to combine the two into a union station linked to the city with a grand boulevard. The THB opted instead to simply elevate its tracks, and build a new facility near the old.

While CN's architect, John Schofield, clung to the more traditional classical lines which his railway was placing in Halifax, Saint John and Edmonton, the THB hired the leading-edge New York firm of Fellheimer and Wagner. This firm had earned a reputation for bold new station designs including the skyscraper style of Buffalo's station, and the bandshell shape of the Cincinnati station.

In 1930 the architects unveiled their plans for Hamilton's new structure. Like Manhattan's skyscrapers, the ten storey tower displayed stepped-back upper stories flanked by low wings at each side, and was ornamented with vertical buttresses. However, hard times forced even the THB to scale back their design and two years later they emerged with a station which was shorter and sleeker. Now only seven stories, it fell within the radically new Art Deco style known as Streamlined Moderne. Adopting the aerodynamic forms of the new age, it showed off smooth wall surfaces and wraparound windows. Inside, steel was used extensively for counters, railings and light fixtures.

It was the only station in this style ever built in Canada to such a scale. Meanwhile, to avoid time consuming, and illegal blockages of its level crossings, the railway elevated its entire line through downtown Hamilton, crossing most roads now on overpasses.

For half a century, Hamiltonians would enter the two storey waiting room through double glass doors. Above them an open mezzanine gallery lined the north side, while on the south a pair of ramps lead up to the tracks. They walked over a beige and brown terrazzo floor or leaned against steel covered columns. On the tracks above, trains departed daily for Toronto, Buffalo, Welland and Brantford. In the offices above were the operational and head office staff of what was truly Hamilton's railway.

But the era would end in 1981 when the CPR took over full operation of the THB and ended passenger service. Most of the railway employees were moved out and the building fell into disrepair. The company even declined grants and loans from the city to help repair it.

Then in 1995 a new era dawned. Hamilton City and GO Transit acquired the building, cleaned and repaired the exterior, restored the lower two floors to their original lustre and reopened the station as a GO Transit terminal and regional bus depot. The ramps to the tracks have been replaced by stairs which are open only during morning and evening train times. Above the waiting room, the second floor mezzanine displays archival images depicting the history of Hamilton's railway. Once more Hamiltonians can enjoy both the beauty and the history of its bold new station and the railway which built it.

The station is situated at the corner of James and Hunter Streets.

HAVELOCK
A Southern Railway Town

The very dominant station on the main street of Havelock is a fitting symbol of the only true railway divisional town south of the Canadian Shield. In the 1880s when the Ontario and Quebec Railway was being surveyed across the middle of Ontario from Toronto to Smiths Falls, a tiny mill village named Havelock stood at the halfway point and was selected as the railway's divisional point.

A large area of flat land close to a supply of water was ideal for the yards and for the steam engines. The town was laid in the grid pat-

A Toronto-bound dayliner prepares to make one of its last departures.

tern of streets more typical of northern divisional towns like Cartier and White River. In true divisional town fashion, the main street developed behind the station with stores, cafes and a pair of hotels.

Havelock's first station was identical to every other station on this railway, save those at Yorkville (Toronto) and Peterborough. They were simple two storey boxes with gable ends and were made of wood; all of them have been removed except the Tweed station. The style was nicknamed the "Van Horne" after the CPR's feisty builder who felt that such buildings were the cheapest and fastest to construct.

The entire town either worked for, or was dependent upon, the CPR whose freights and passenger trains puffed through at a rate of 14 every day. One of these was the "meat train" which, to prevent spoilage, was "highballed" through from the stock yards of Chicago to the markets and restaurants of New York.

Then, in 1912, word came with a shudder that the CPR was about to build a new main line along the shore of Lake Ontario. Worried residents and politicians lobbied the government to prevent what they feared would be the end of Havelock.

However, instead of abandoning its divisional town, the CPR announced plans for a new station, along with a sand tower, a coal elevator, and an expansion to the roundhouse. A dozen years would pass, however, before a revised station plan was unveiled, and construction started.

Finally, in 1929, the new station was opened. It was, however, an era which no longer saw elaborate and fanciful stations coming from the offices of the railway architects. Small town stations would now be simple and functional, and that was the case with the new Havelock station.

Using brick upon a concrete foundation, the station, while simple, was distinctive and dominant. The storey and a half Tudor Revival building displayed cross gables which covered bays located on each side of the station. The waiting room measured 36 feet by 19 feet (roughly 12m by 6 m) with smaller adjoining women's rest rooms and a men's smoking room. All were finished in quarter cut oak, with paneled walls, a coved ceiling and terrazzo floors. Even the washrooms were elegantly finished in marble with tile floors.

The station also had enough room for the yard staff, conductors and trainmen, as well as private rooms for the superintendent and his assistant. A planned restaurant was scrapped in favour of a news, tobacco and candy stand in one corner of the waiting area. Beside the station a garden stretched to the west.

While much has changed, the area around the station still retains its railway related landscapes. South of the station the vast yards are still filled with ore cars and engines, while behind the station the main street remains lined with many of the early hotels and cafes. Similarly, much of the interior has been little altered.

Such cannot be said for the OQR itself. When the controversial lakeshore line opened, the OQR, as expected, lost traffic. That portion of the line between Glen Tay and Tweed, the easternmost portion, was abandoned in 1971, while the western section between Tweed and Blairton was lifted in 1987, and the line now only extends a couple of km east of Havelock. A pair of nepheline cyanite mines several km to the north provide the sole life support for the railway operations. The last passenger train to Toronto ran in 1990 when it was eliminated by the federal government under Brain Mulroney. More recently the federal ministry of transport has indicated its wish to see that service restored, perhaps as a part of the GO Transit service from Toronto.

Although the CPR continued to use the station until recently, it has been sold to private interests who have yet to reveal plans for it. The station and the yards are beside Highway 7 in the heart of the community. A newly landscaped parking area, with a railway-themed information office, has taken over the grounds of the former garden west of the station.

HORNEPAYNE
Still a Railway Town

Unlike most of northern Ontario's early railway towns, Hornepayne remains almost all railway. The town came to life when William Mackenzie and Donald Mann completed the missing link in their cross-Canada Canadian Northern Railway through the area. It was to be the final stage of their ambitious line, connecting Thunder Bay with Ottawa.

Thanks to the level terrain and the presence of water, this Cree hunting ground was selected for a divisional point. The first station

Although the horse-drawn carts are gone, the Hornepayne station remains a focus of railway activity.

was a standard storey-and-a-half CNo station and was accompanied by an 18 stall roundhouse, a restaurant and employee housing. A grid pattern of streets was laid out behind the station, and the town of "Fitzback" was born. The name was soon changed to honour Robert Montgomery Hornepayne, a key financial backer of the railway.

By 1919 the CNR had been created to take over bankrupt lines like the Canadian Northern, and began improvements to the line. When the roundhouse burned in 1919, it was replaced with a state of the art, "indoor" roundhouse. Then in 1921 the CNo station was replaced with a larger two-storey brick station. Because this was a functional railway town, ornamentation was not needed to attract passengers. The building was unadorned by gables, or fretwork, nor did it adhere to any trendy architectural theme. In appearance, the station was all business. Nearly identical stations were built at Armstrong (extant but vandalized) and Capreol (replaced), both of which were divisional points. Capreol, like Hornepayne, remains a busy railway centre.

Although little passenger traffic was generated from Hornepayne, being a divisional point, through passengers would disembark for the time the train was being serviced and adequate space was needed for that. At 21' by 31' (7m by 10m), the general waiting room was not especially large. Instead, many headed for the restaurant or "Beanery" as it was affectionately called where they would gobble a hasty meal at a horseshoe-shaped counter.

Although the town remains a busy railway town, the station was closed in the 1980s when VIA erected a small shelter, and the CN moved into new office facilities. The building remains vacant and has been vandalized. Although it is designated under the HRSPA, there are no plans either by the railway or the town to re-use it.

Hornepayne has two other unusual buildings, both railway-related. In the 1980s a proposal was put forward to place the entire town under one roof. Given the long and bitter winters which plague the area, this didn't seem like such a bad idea. Thus was born the

Hornepayne Hallmark Centre. Within this single building are nine provincial government ministries, four federal agencies, a hotel, a dozen stores, a high school, a gym, a swimming pool, seniors' apartments, as well as offices and bachelor apartments for CN employees.

The other is the historic roundhouse. At 223' by 287' (72m by 95m) it is the last indoor roundhouse in the world. The interior contains an 80' (26m) turntable with 16 eight-foot (2.5m) engine pits. Again, the severe cold necessitated such an unusual adaptation.

As in the days of Mackenzie and Mann, Hornepayne remains relatively remote. Although it lies on a highway, the route, halfway between the two Trans Canada highways, is only lightly travelled. That, however, has only helped enhance the aura of this living railway legacy.

Hornepayne lies on the lonely Highway 631 about midway between Highways 11 and 17.

While large, the Hornepayne station can boast of few architectural embellishments.

HUNTSVILLE
Will the Trains Still Call?

Even though it was not an architecturally ornamented station to begin with, the CN's Huntsville station is in pretty sorry shape now. While structurally still sound, its maintenance has been neglected, and its overall appearance is unkempt.

The station was built at a time when the era of building grand stations was ending. It replaced an earlier two storey wooden station in 1924, and was more functional than fanciful.

The railways first reached Huntsville in 1885 when the rails of the

The Huntsville station is much less busy than when it was first built.

Trackmen make repairs in front of the Huntsville station in the days of steam.

Northern and North Western Railway were laid along the shores of Lake Vernon. From the station passengers could board the steamers and sail for one of the many burgeoning Muskoka resorts. A system of canals was built to link the town with Mary, Fairy and Peninsula Lakes, while a short portage railway provided further access to the steamers on Lake of Bays.

The first station was built to a standard two-storey design used by the railway and was found in places like Beeton, Burk's Falls and Bracebridge. A similar structure still stands at Coldwater. With its board and batten siding and high hipped gable at the ends, it was a simple but attractive structure. Because of the hilly configuration of the town, the station location was not influential in shaping Huntsville's growth. Nonetheless, the town could not have existed without it.

But by the 1920s the CN had taken over the GT, along with Canada's other bankrupt rail lines, and was more interested in getting the railway on its feet financially than it was in building elaborate stations. With the absorption of the Grand Trunk into the CN, both passenger and freight service increased, and new yards and station were needed. Built of brick, the new station offered a steep but plain roofline. Inside, most of the space was given over to a general waiting room, although there was a separate rest area for ladies.

Many of the original yard buildings such as agent's house, section dwellings, stock yard and tool houses were all removed when the yard improvements occurred. The only building to date to the early days was the hotel at the top of the hill above the station, which originally served as a boarding house for the train crews.

Most of the industries served by the railway have gone as well and at this writing the Ontario government is threatening to terminate the last of the passenger trains. Until then, the tiny waiting room remains sparsely furnished, while the exterior paint job continues to fade, and potholes plague the small parking area. Still, Huntsville remains a popular boarding spot for summer cottagers who want to avoid the weekend road congestion, and for fall excursionists who can gape at the spectacular forest colours of Muskoka and Parry Sound from the comfort of a train seat.

The residents of the town are concerned about the fate of their station and, in response, council has designated it as a heritage structure while beautifying the grounds nearby. There has been private interest in the building, but that interest would depend upon whether or not rail passenger service continues. At present, the ONR's *Northlander* passenger train still calls here twice a day, once in each direction.

The station can be found at the foot of a steep hill at the west end of the main street.

Railway heritage of a different stripe has also resurfaced in the town, with the restoration of the old Portage Railway equipment beside the Muskoka Pioneer Village located on Brunel Road.

GRAVENHURST

Although Huntsville was the only station on the former Grand Trunk route between Orillia and North Bay to be federally designated, three other stations still stand and offer heritage value: Gravenhurst, South River and Washago. Because the Gravenhurst station was successfully preserved as part of an experimental Ontario Ministry of Transportation program, it was not eligible for designation under the HRSPA.

Built in the early 1900s, it was the second station to be located in Gravenhurst.

Most Muskoka vacationers think of Gravenhurst's heritage in terms of its handsome opera house, or its popular steam ship the RMS Segwun. Few remember the town's railway roots. Yet it was here that vacation trains would puff onto the Muskoka wharf where vaca-

It took a community effort to revitalize the Gravenhurst station. The *Northlander* is pulling up to the platform to pick up the summer crowd.

tioners would board one of the many Muskoka steamers bound for the grand hotels which ringed the lakes.

Gravenhurst was also a divisional point on the Northern and North Western Railway which linked Atherley Junction on Lake Simcoe with Callander on Lake Nipissing. Then, when the Grand Trunk assumed this link and extended its service to the NTR at Cochrane, the stations along the line were either upgraded or replaced.

The first Gravenhurst station was a two-storey barn-like structure closer to the yards, now long gone, which lay at the south end of town. The new station, however, was better situated to serve the downtown core. The station complex consisted of three buildings, the waiting room and agency, the most northerly of the three, immediately south of that was the express and baggage shed, while the third housed a restaurant.

In 1983 the station became the subject of a Ministry of Transportation program to convert selected rail passenger stations into multi-modal terminals. (Nakina and Orillia were two others). When the project was completed in 1986, the ticketing office had acquired the snack bar, while the two ancillary buildings were leased out as commercial or municipal space.

At that time, four trains still called daily, two operated by VIA Rail, and two by the Ontario Northland, while regional buses pulled in at the rear of the building. The buses still call, but the train service is now down to the twice daily *Northlander* which, at this writing, may be put up for sale.

The attractive station is a white wooden structure on a stone foundation with an octagonal waiting room which faces northward up the track. It is complemented by an octagonal operator's bay surmounted by a hip gable. On the street side a pair of eyelid-shaped dormers punctuate the roofline.

The station remains a focus of community activity and, like that at Huntsville, is a popular boarding point for rail travellers, especially during the summer, who prefer the comfort of rail travel over the congestion of the roads. It is close to both the downtown core, with its heritage streetscape, and to the popular Gull Lake park, at the corner of Brock Street and Bethune Drive.

SOUTH RIVER

The only remaining station stop between Huntsville and North Bay is at South River. It is also the sole surviving example of a station built by the original railway company, in this case the Northern and Northwestern Railway. Like Gravenhurst, South River was given the status of a divisional point. The station was originally located on the east side of the yards, opposite the town, where a roundhouse, section houses, water tower, and coal chute were added.

The town itself grew along Ottawa Avenue on the west side of the

The only original station on the Huntsville line, the station at South River needs some improvements.

tracks. When the Grand Trunk acquired the NNW, it moved the station closer to the town, and enlarged it. Unlike the standard NNW station plans, which displayed steeply pitched roofs with hipped end gables, that at South River had a shallower pitch with dormers above the ends and the operators bay. The small waiting room occupied the north end of the building.

South River lacked a station restaurant which was a fixture at most divisional points. Instead, patrons would simply pass through the station to where the Queens and King Edward hotels stood close by on Ottawa Ave.

By the end of World War II most of the divisional buildings had been removed. The section houses had either burned or were moved; the roundhouse had burned along with the original coal chute in 1932. While the latter was replaced, and still stands, the roundhouse was not. Finally the station itself was closed in 1986 and boarded up. Although considered for Federal designation, it was rejected.

In 1998 a local group of citizens formed a "save the station" committee and received a grant from the Northen Ontario Heritage fund. At this writing, a library facility, among other uses, is being considered for the building. As long as the service remains available, it also remains a station stop for the Ontario government's *Northlander* train.

South River lies on Highway 11 approximately 50 km south of North Bay. Ottawa Avenue runs east of the highway in the centre of the village.

WASHAGO

Eyebrows might rise at the distance which the Washago station is set back from the railway tracks. But that was not always the case. The station never moved, however the tracks did.

When the NNW built its line linking Atherley with Callander, the tracks passed immediately to the east of the station. The present building is the second station to occupy the site, the original having stood on the east side of the tracks. In 1913 when the Canadian Northern

The tracks on which the Washago station were built have been moved.

Railway built its Toronto to Sudbury line, Washago became a junction between that line and what had by then become the Grand Trunk, and the present station was built. Although it was located on the Grand Trunk track, it was built to a Canadian Northern pattern found also at the now relocated stations which served Richmond Hill and Mount Albert. Nearly identical to the Grand Trunk's "stick style" stations found at Newmarket, Aurora and Maple, the CNo pattern at Washago is differentiated by a shallower pitch to the roof and the gables.

Although it was not a divisional point, as a busy junction it gained yards, a water tower and a coal chute. To accommodate the widening of Highway 11 in the 1970s, and eliminate the need for a second crossing, the former GT track was relocated to follow the Canadian Northern trackage for a short distance west of the original junction site. The tracks which abutted the station on the east were lifted as far as the new junction, giving the station its unusual set-back aspect.

The station was closed to passengers in 1978 and replaced with a shelter. Now extensively altered, and covered with aluminum siding, the building is still used by CN maintenance crews. Today a shelter is provided for passengers using VIA Rail's popular *Canadian* which follows the old CNo route to Sudbury, and for those using the ONR's daily *Northlander*, which follows the former Grand Trunk line to North Bay.

While the water tower was remodelled in metal, the coal chute, like that at South River, still stands, a vestige of the landscape from a disappearing era.

Washago is located east of Highway 11 about 25 km north of Orillia.

KENORA
A Northern Chateau

Although many visitors to Kenora are drawn by the beauty of the Lake of the Woods beside which it sits, the town owes its origins to the railway. When the CPR was building its all-Canadian route in the 1880s, it selected this location as a divisional point. A small wooden station was opened by the yards which lay a short distance to the north and east of the town. Grain, lumber and gold at the time were the main revenue generators for the railway.

The Kenora station is one the CPR's most elaborate Chateauesque stations.

But the CPR's chief builder, William Cornelius Van Horne, was one of the first railwaymen to realize the tourism potential of the land through which his railway ran. He exploited this in the Rockies with the construction of the Banff Springs hotel and later the Chateau Lake Louise. Elaborate stations at these two locations reinforced the railway's urge to draw tourists.

Shortly after the line through Kenora had opened, railway executives from Winnipeg had begun to spend their summer weekends on the Lake of the Woods. Anxious to expand its tourism appeal the railway built a lodge of its own on an island in the lake, as well as a grand hotel in town, and then began to design a station which would be its most attractive in northern Ontario. By the time the new Kenora station was finished in 1899, it looked more like a chateau, or a "Swiss chalet" as the local newspaper described it, than a typical railway station.

The first thing one notices is the roof line. Above the street entrance loomed a central tower capped by a six-sided conical roof. Another tower dominated the track side, both of which were flanked by hooded gables. The windows and doors were topped with arches, while the whole structure was built of local brick resting on top of granite. Inside were a large general waiting room, and ladies' waiting room along with baggage and express rooms, and the usual restaurant. Residential space was provided upstairs for the agent and other employees. Because the CPR wanted to give tourists a grand first impression of the town, they laid out one of their most elaborate gardens, complete with a fountain. The station was one the CPR's showpieces.

As for more functional railway structures, there were a roundhouse, water tower, coal shed and to the south a railway YMCA to house the crews.

While tourists still flock to Kenora, nowadays they drive. Passenger service was curtailed in 1990 by the federal government under Brian Mulroney, and the station's interior was completely altered to make room for more offices. The roof line was altered to provide for a full second floor, although the steep pitch and the towers still survive. The wonderful gardens are gone now, too, replaced by parking lots and commercial development.

While the station remains a divisional point on the CPR, its maintenance has slipped and its ambience has dissipated. Nevertheless, the local populace remains very much attached to this most vital piece of their built heritage and are determined that it should survive. It is located two blocks north of the town hall which stands on the main street.

VIA's *Canadian* no longer stops at the Kenora station.

KINGSTON
Trackless Then and Now

The old stone station at Kingston may be the only such facility to have served as a station before the tracks appeared and to still be in use even after they were removed.

When the Grand Trunk was constructing its lines in the early 1850s, the project was carried out in three sections. One involved construction from Montreal towards Brockville, the second from Toronto to Oshawa, while the third segment originated in Kingston

The Grand Trunk's historic Kingston station before the tracks were lifted and fire damaged the interior.

and led both east and west to meet the others. To provide a headquarters for the planning and building of the third phase, the GT in
1855 built a storey and a half stone station three miles (5 km) north
of Kingston.

A year later the tracks were completed and the trains began to
arrive. At first the Kingston station closely resembled 34 other stone
or brick way stations along the line. These buildings were wide with
a low roof line and distinguished by the row of arched French doors
along both sides and the ends. Larger stations were those with seven
arches on each side, the smaller sported five. The design originated
with an 1840s station in Kenilworth, England.

Because administration offices required were at Kingston, the
building, unlike the others, was given a second floor. Sometime
between 1876 and 1885, the second floor roof was enlarged through
the construction of a mansard roof.

It had been the GT's policy to compete with, and not cooperate
with, great lakes shippers and for this reason they located their stations well inland. This would allow them to intercept goods from the
hinterland which would otherwise have been destined for the
wharves on the lake. But Kingston's harbour was too important to
ignore for long, and by 1895 the GT had extended a spur line to the
docks and built a ticket office there as well. This addition was
spurred on by the construction of the rival Kingston and Pembroke
Railway in 1886 and its wharfside station opposite the City Hall.

Because of its distance from downtown Kingston, a community
grew around what now became known as the "outer" station with a
string of houses known as Grand Trunk terrace. Other buildings
around the station included two engine houses, a freight house and
a "refreshment saloon" which sat on the north side of the tracks.

By the 1890s the GT was serving passengers from a number of
other railway lines as well, including the Bay of Quinte, the Napanee
and Tamworth and the Kingston and Pembroke railways, and the
yards were enlarged. The old "saloon" was removed and replaced
with a brick restaurant east of the station. Later, the station facilities

were moved into the restaurant, and the original station was converted to offices.

Then in 1983, when the CN decided to eliminate the sharp bend in the tracks on which the station sat and thereby straighten its alignment, the old station was again left trackless. Even though a new passenger facility was built on the new track on Princess Street north, the old building continued to function as CN's regional headquarters until 1987, when it was declared surplus. For a time a restaurant occupied the buildings, but now they sit vacant, fire scarred, and surrounded by a trackless wasteland.

Meanwhile, Kingston's other two historic stations have enjoyed gainful re-use, the GT downtown station as a restaurant at King and Johnson St, and the K and P station, opposite the City Hall, as an information office.

Kingston's "outer" station and the station restaurant are on the west side of Montreal Street between Hickson and Elliot.

BROCKVILLE

Although it was not accorded a heritage designation under the HRSPA, the divisional station at Brockville does, nonetheless, mark a key historic divisional point on the old Grand Trunk railway line between Kingston and Montreal.

Brockville's first station was located on the south side of the tracks at the north end of Buell Street and resembled the usual square, low-roofed pattern found frequently along the line. But in 1872, with traffic increasing, and with a new line open between Brockville and Ottawa, a larger facility was needed. The new station, which in style was an elongated version of the old one, was built on the north side of the tracks. With the CPR's Ottawa tracks on the north side of the building, and those of the GT on the south, the location was considered a "union" station.

The yard buildings included an engine house, roundhouse, road-master stores, coal sheds, ice house, cattle pens and a large freight

The Grand Trunk station in Brockville is one of VIA Rail's busiest.

shed. With the end of the steam era, Brockville ceased to serve as a divisional point and most of the yard buildings were removed. The only ancillary structure to survive to the present is the 1929 yard office located east of the current station.

The station, brick on a stone foundation, with a string of arched doors and windows, has been extensively altered, the original exterior now obscured by aluminum siding. Nevertheless, a small garden is still maintained beside the station, and VIA Rail's trains still call here 18 times a day on both the Toronto-Montreal and Toronto-Ottawa runs.

GANANOQUE JUNCTION

While this little turreted station may not have been designated under the HRSPA, it was a part of Ontario's shortest railway, the Thousands Islands Railway.

Angered that the Grand Trunk had located their station at so great a distance from their community, 8 km to the south, the residents of Gananoque on the St Lawrence for years relentlessly lobbied for a rail link to the main line. That finally happened in 1889 when the Rathbun Company of Deseronto, builders of the Bay of Quinte Railway, came to their rescue and constructed the short line.

Surprisingly, the line quickly became a popular destination for tourists wishing to visit the Thousand Islands area. Anxious to reap the bounty from the growing tourist trade, the Grand Trunk leased the line for itself, eventually purchasing it outright.

A VIA train slips past the Gananoque Junction station. Only two still stop here each day.

In part to improve train operations (the original Gananoque station was in a poor location) and in part to attract tourists, the GT relocated the junction and built a new station. Although small, the new building displayed a decorative central tower, and a varied roofline. Attractive gardens surrounded the structure. A new satellite village grew around the station and was named Gananoque Junction, while that which had existed around the old facility, Cheeseboro, became a ghost town.

The GT also built a new tourist station by the wharf on the river where tourists could buy cruise tickets and board the boats right there. On the main street of the town was a decorative little "umbrella" station.

Passenger service on the TIR stopped in 1962. The wharf station burned in 1990 and the tracks of Ontario's shortest railway were lifted soon after. The "umbrella" station still stands, trackless, on Gananoque's main street, while the refurbished junction station is now a VIA station with trains calling twice daily. It is located on Station Rd east of Leeds County Road 43.

KITCHENER
They Took Away the Tower

The simple station that stands in Kitchener today bears little resemblance to its original appearance. In 1856 Berlin, as it was called then, was largely a German town surrounded by a community of Mennonite farmers. In that year, the GTR reached neighbouring Guelph from which it was connected to Berlin by the locally built Toronto Guelph and Berlin Railway. A small station was built near Market Street, then the main thoroughfare from the farmlands to the north, and the street beside it was named Gzowski Street. These streets today are respectively Weber

An early postcard view shows the tower which once dominated the Kitchener station.

Street and Edward Street. Gzowski Street was named in honour of Sir Casimir Gzowski, chief engineer of the Grand Trunk Railway, and great-grandfather to the late broadcaster, Peter Gzowski.

Then, in 1895, spurred on by the Laurier government's free trade policy with the U.S., the GT's new president, Charles Melville Hays, undertook to upgrade the line's tracks and stations. New stations were built between 1891 and 1911 at Sarnia, Grimsby, Goderich, Brantford, Brampton, Guelph and Stratford. All except the one at Grimsby survive.

Up until that point, Berlin's industrial base was largely derived from its prosperous farming hinterland, and the processing, storing and shipping of farm products. But the revamped GT would change all that. In 1897, responding to the opportunities offered by free trade, Berlin's promoters began to lobby the GT for a new station.

Their efforts soon paid off. In 1896 GT architect Joseph Hobson designed for the town a new rectangular station fairly simple in its design. But because station towers had become a symbol of a community's importance, and a trend in U.S. stations, Berlin insisted on a tower on theirs. The GT acquiesced and the following year Hobson revised the design to include a prominent tower above the operator's bay.

The roof line also included a large gable above the entrance and smaller dormers on both the east and west parts of the roof. Following a fire in 1908 a second tower was added to one corner of the building. An arched porte-cochere was placed over the platform at the west end of the station where a door led to the general waiting room. The ladies' waiting room was situated in the lower portion of the corner tower. In 1925 a freight building was built to the east of the station.

But the landscape around the station was changing too. With access to the U.S through Laurier's free trade, Berlin began to add factories producing products which ranged from furniture and pianos to buttons, boots and bows. Many of these were located right beside the tracks. In fact one new factory, the Berlin Furniture Factory, was built between the station and Victoria St, visually cutting the station off from the rest of the community. In contrast to the factories, an

Although still a train stop, the Kitchener station has been shorn of its architectural embellishments.

attractive brick hotel was built just steps from the covered platform.

Then, in 1966, CN, which had assumed control of the GT in 1923, decided to "modernize" the station. While windows and doors were replaced, the entire roof lost its features completely. The towers and dormers were ripped out leaving only the simple unembellished roofline which the station offers today.

The interior features were covered over with drop ceilings and wall paneling while the doors to the covered platform were filled in. Modernization had obliterated the architectural beauty of Hobson's original design and the city in effect lost the station which it had lobbied so hard to obtain.

Then, when the CN withdrew from passenger service in 1983, it threatened to demolish the station. VIA Rail, however, opted to retain the building. They also undertook improvements including relocating the ticket window, adding glassed-in vestibules to the entrances, and converting the baggage room to an employees' lounge.

Although the station itself has been much altered, little has changed around it. Factories still line the tracks to the north, although many are now closed. The hotel, too, still functions as a popular grill and tavern. Despite being on a heavily urbanized corridor, only five passenger trains a day provide service from the Kitchener station. (Although, as of this writing, additional service is being proposed)

The station is located near the intersection of Weber and Victoria Streets in downtown Kitchener.

Joseph Hobson's 1897 plans for the Kitchener station reveal a far more pleasing style than that which survives today.

MAPLE
A Rural Oasis

Toronto's urban sprawl has over-whelmed the one-time farm towns of Maple and Richmond Hill, and is fast filling the gap between them. A visit to the Maple station becomes like a step back in time, a visual refuge from the traffic and the sprawl.

That is all largely due to the station's location. When the Ontario Simcoe and Huron Railway was first opened in 1853, it was Ontario's first railway, and its "Richmond Hill" station was more than 5.5 miles

The Maple station stands in a rural oasis surrounded by an encroaching urban fringe.

(9 km) west of the village which it was intended to serve. Such separation was caused by the steep hills of the Oak Ridge moraine upon which Richmond Hill was built. Meanwhile, an inconsequential little crossroads hamlet named Maple lay a short distance to the west.

Although Richmond Hill lobbied hard for a connecting spur, they failed to offer any financial incentive, and the spur was never built. This inaction led to the demise of a promising village between Maple and Richmond Hill. Patterson began in 1850 as farm implement factory. A village soon grew around the factory and included a large boarding house and 25 single dwellings. But the failure of the spur line, and the promise

The interior of the Maple station has been restored with history in mind.

of funding from Woodstock, prompted the factory to move to that location, and Patterson became a ghost town. The remnants survive today and include the factory, boarding house, first owner's mansion, and three of the 25 dwellings.

With the arrival of the railway Maple grew modestly. Farmers would ship out produce from the station while a small number of passengers would embark. By 1890, the line, now the Northern Railway, had been extended to both Collingwood on Georgian Bay, and to Callander on Lake Nipissing. In 1903, the original Northern station burned and Grand Trunk, which had control of the Northern by this time, replaced it with a contemporary pattern of its own.

Built in dozens of locations around the province, the style was known as the "stick" style. It incorporated decorative gables at both ends and above the operator's bay. Within those gables were highly decorative fretwork, scrolled bargeboard, and basketweave trellis patterns. The exterior woodwork consisted of ornamental patterns of vertical, horizontal and diagonal boards.

Because the station was of little more than local importance to the railway, the interior was divided simply into the standard three components, the waiting room, the baggage room and between them the agent's office and ticket wicket.

Its modest role left the area around the station only lightly developed, with agent's house, freight house, operator's house and stable. Otherwise, the grounds were surrounded by farms.

During the 1990s GO Transit acquired the building and restored its exterior, repainting it from faded white to red and yellow, the traditional colours of the Grand Trunk. While much of the inside was gutted to provide for waiting commuters, the use of decorative woodwork successfully recalls the flavour of the period. Perhaps the most sensitive part of the preservation effort was the retention of the mileage board. In 1997 CN lifted the trackage between Barrie and Orillia, thus severing the line's link to CN's main line and today's train traffic consists almost solely of daily GO trains.

West of Maple, housing subdivisions stretch to the horizon. To the immediate east loom the mountains of garbage in the Keele Landfill Site, scheduled for closing in 2004. East of that again, Richmond Hill's urban fringe stands poised to leap onto even more farmland.

Yet the little Maple station seems remote from all that. Although the related buildings have all been removed, and the grounds taken over by a commuter parking lot, the site remains one of relative tranquility.

The station is situated on Hill Street north of Major Mackenzie Drive a short distance east of the railway underpass.

MARKHAM
Open for Business Again

Even though construction fencing still cluttered the platform, Markham's dignitaries gathered around the red ribbon. Mayor Don Cousens looked toward the waiting cameras and snipped. Thus, in September of 2001, the revitalized Markham train station was officially reopened for business.

More than 130 years had passed since the first train of the Toronto and Nipissing Railway puffed past on its way to Uxbridge Ontario. In 1868 when the T and N came looking for money to help finance the line, the residents of the township of Markham approved a sub-

Markham station has now been carefully restored to its original appearance.

sidy of $30,000, but they wanted two stations, not one, for both the village of Markham and the village of Unionville.

Although the railway never made it to Nipissing, it did reach Coboconk. Later, under the Midland Railway, it was extended to Lindsay and Peterborough from which point the Grand Junction provided service to Belleville. Passengers could therefore wait on the platform of the Markham station and at 6:24pm board east bound train number 94. Four and half hours later they would disembark at Belleville.

As was the practice of most railway companies, the T and N, to avoid higher land costs, laid their line well away from the village, near the rural hamlet of Mount Joy. At that time, Markham consisted of fewer than 1000 residents clustered around the grist mills on the Rouge River. But with the construction of the new station, industries made their way to trackside, and included foundries, woolen mills and farm implement factories. By 1915 both communities had grown together and Mount Joy was annexed to Markham.

Markham's station was simple in its design. Long and low, it lacked architectural embellishments. Passengers waited in the northeast end of the buildings, while baggage and freight facilities occupied the southwest end. In between was the agent's office and communications facilities.

Markham's station is one of the few first generation stations in Ontario still on its original site. Like most, it was built to a standard pattern. The style could be found at other stations along the line including Goodwood, Sunderland and Cannington. Although local newspapers called for its replacement as early as 1898, the light traffic on the line did not warrant the expense.

Over the years, the building suffered from poor alterations and neglect. Floors were covered with linoleum tiles, new counters added and a small washroom installed. According to one report, it had been "crudely altered, poorly reclad and badly maintained." Critics deplored the deferred maintenance and inappropriate reclamation work such as the "abysmal" siding which covered the original materials and details.

By the mid-1980s all the tracks beyond Uxbridge were gone. The Markham station was never without service, however, as commuter trains continued to operate to Stouffville. With the station then closed to rail service, Markham's passengers were required to use a small wooden shelter.

Thanks to a concerned citizenry and council, the station at Markham has been restored to the appearance shown in this early view, minus the horses.

But the Town of Markham and the Markham Conservancy acquired the vacant building and, along with GO Transit, have restored the station to much of its original grandeur. With funding from the federal Millennium Fund and local contributions, the Town upgraded the inside and restored the outside. While the interior is modernized to accommodate meetings and handicap access, the outside once more displays much of the detailing which passengers would have seen a hundred years ago, including the name board, signage, and even the chalk timetable. The insulbrick covering has been tossed away, and the yellow and green paint scheme once more shines in the afternoon sun.

The parking lot is filled with commuter vehicles, and four times a day GO trains squeal to a halt by the station platform. Of these trains two continue to Stouffville.

On Stouffville's main street a new station was built, not just for GO travellers, but for heritage enthusiasts who can board the historic coaches of the York and Durham Heritage Railway and travel 11 miles (18 km) further on to the restored station at Uxbridge. Now a museum, this wooden station was the grandest on the T and N, sporting the rather more elaborate "witch's hat" conical roof above the waiting room.

NAKINA
Built by Silk

It would not be too great an exaggeration to claim that the Nakina station was built by silk. In 1923 the newly-formed and government-owned Canadian National Railway found itself in possession of two bankrupt railway lines through northern Ontario. The former Canadian Northern Railway looped eastward from Port Arthur and then north through Geraldton and Longlac, and then bent back southeasterly through Hornepayne and Sudbury and on to Toronto. The former Grand Trunk Pacific passed to the north through Sioux Lookout, Armstrong and Cochrane before making its way to Quebec City.

The remote divisional station at Nakina has since been converted to a multi-modal facility.

Even though they passed within 42 km of each other at one point, there was no connection between the two. Henry Thornton, CN's brilliant president, was determined that taxpayers would not be burdened with these money-losing operations. To earn the much-needed revenue, he negotiated a contract to haul precious Japanese silk from the west coast to New York. But silk deteriorates quickly, and a faster route was needed to secure the lucrative deal. To reduce the travelling time by a precious four hours, Thornton proposed a link between the two closest points on the parallel routes, the logging town of Longlac on the former CNo, and the railway's divisional town of Grant on the GTP.

But by the time the 28 miles (42 km) link was finished, Grant lay too far east of the junction to continue its railway role, and Thornton opted to move the town. And so in 1923, train and construction crews disassembled a 950 square foot store house, a 12 stall roundhouse, a 1600 square foot rest house, and a 70,000 gallon water tank, placed them all on specially designed flat cars and hauled them 27 km west along the track to the new junction where they reassembled them.

The new site was named Nakina, meaning "meeting place," and surveyed into a townsite. The main street lay behind the station, while a street lined with workers' homes led down to the tracks. Totally isolated, as were most of northern Ontario's early divisional towns, Nakina depended completely upon the CNR both for jobs and access to the world outside.

The station was a very functional building. A storey and half high, it was constructed of wood on a concrete foundation. No ornamentation decorated the shallow hip roof, no gables protruded above the windows or the operator's bay. Inside, the central portion was made up of the general waiting room, with a ladies' waiting room to the side. A baggage room lay at the west end, while a 23 stool lunch counter occupied the east end.

The second floor was comprised of quarters for the agent and his family at one end, while at the other were accommodations for other railway personnel.

The 1950s marked a decade of change for the town. A new highway opened up in 1956 linking the community by road for the first time to Geraldton on the Trans Canada Highway. Then, when the railways switched from steam to diesel, the need for divisional points was drastically reduced, as were the number of jobs in most of them. In the 1960s when CN announced it was going to run their trains right through Nakina entirely, railway workers across Canada staged a strike to protest job losses, and the possible end to a community as well.

Another 20 years would pass before CN followed through on the change. By then Nakina enjoyed a paved road to Geraldton and an airport as well. Tourists were discovering that the community was a gateway to remote hunting and fishing areas further north, while mining and logging filled in the jobs lost by the railway. Its station, however, stood vacant and vandalized, its paint peeling, and there was only an unheated and foul-smelling waiting area for the few passengers who would board here.

While the yards are now empty, and most of the old stores on the main street been removed or replaced, the station has been revitalized. Using a now-discontinued funding program provided by the Ontario Ministry of Transportation and Communications, the exterior has been repainted, and the shattered windows have been replaced. Today the building has become a multi-modal and community facility, complete with a new restaurant.

Even though the freights rumble right on past, VIA Rail's *Canadian* still stops six times a week to board fishers, hunters and native Ojibway travelling to their remote trackside villages.

The village lies at the end of Highway 584 about 38 miles (60 km) north of Geraldton. And that makes it still pretty remote.

NEWMARKET
Out of Place Now

Newmarket's Grand Trunk railway station and its environs makes for a study in contrasts. Surrounded by the urban sprawl and landscape disfigurements of the rapidly growing town of Newmarket, the old wooden station looks decidedly out of place.

It was built in 1904 to a pattern which was then in wide use. By the end of the 19th century, the Grand Trunk had acquired 49 small-

The Newmarket station before the surrounding development and the end of its train service.

er lines across the country and, under the leadership of Charles Hayes, began a programme of upgrading. Many of the improvements meant replacing earlier stations with structures which were larger and more appealing.

The first station in Newmarket was built by the Ontario Simcoe and Huron, later the Northern Railway, in the 1850s and resembled those at Holland Landing, Concord and King City. The only first generation station to survive from the line is King City. It has been moved to the municipal museum grounds on King Road.

The design of the new building, known as the "stick" style, incorporated gables above the operator's bay and at both ends. Within these gables arches and sunbursts made for aesthetically pleasing decoration. The exterior woodwork was likewise highly decorative, consisting of wainscotting and vertical and diagonal boarding. It was a pattern repeated at dozens of GT stations of that era, and other examples survive at Milton, Stayner and Tecumseh, all now relocated, and at Maple and Aurora, both renovated as GO stations.

Inside the station, the three main rooms were lined with ornately designed Georgia pine trim prompting the Newmarket Era newspaper to call the newly finished station "tasty."

The layout of the building was, as usual, simple, and placed the agent in the middle with separate men's and ladies' waiting areas on either side.

Because Newmarket predated the railway, the location of the station had limited impact on the town's overall shape. It had begun as a Quaker settlement on Yonge St, but developed around mill sites on the Holland River. When the station was built north of the town's core area, the direction of commercial growth moved northward up Main Street toward the station.

In the immediate area of the station grounds, the dominant use was industry, including the large Davis tannery. Eventually the Northern Railroad was extended to North Bay and incorporated into the Grand Trunk's mainline system. Several trains a day stopped at the Newmarket station, including those bound for Canada's west coast.

As Newmarket became a dormitory town to the expanding greater Toronto area, the area around the station changed. Strip malls and parking lots spilled along the roadside, while the railway buildings of another day disappeared from the landscape. On the north side of Davis Dr, the Davis tannery itself was renovated into a mall with a waiting room for GO trains.

During this time, some improvements were made to the station. The insulbrick siding was removed and the original paint scheme of red and yellow restored while the interior was altered to make way for the offices of the local federal member of parliament.

In 1997 when CN lifted the tracks around Lake Simcoe, the status of the line was downgraded to branch line. Today, only GO trains pass the old structure. The MP has moved on, and the station once more sits unused, and decidedly out of place in its suburban environment.

Although the historical preservation record of the town of Newmarket is less than noteworthy, the station has, in addition to its federal heritage designation, been locally designated as a heritage building. It sits on the south side of Davis Street a short distance east of Main Street.

An early view of the Newmarket station when the *Northlander* still called.

NIAGARA FALLS
Take the Train to the Falls

It may come as a surprise to some that the location of the impressive Niagara Falls railway station had nothing to do with the area's major tourist draw, the Falls. Rather, the early railway builders were more interested in competing with the American railway and canal builders and sought the simplest route across the river.

Although built in 1854 by Canadians, the area's first railway, the Great Western, was intended to provide the shortest rail route between the American lines in Michigan and those in New York State. The completion of the line between Niagara Falls and Windsor achieved just that.

Niagara Falls' first station was a low wide board and batten building. A community quickly developed around it and was called Elgin. When the original station burned in 1879 the GW's chief architect, Joseph Hobson, set to work designing one of his many trademark Gothic stations. Two storeys high in the centre, it was balanced by single storey wings at each end. Its steep roof line with equally steep hip gables was Hobson's trademark and this style can also be found at stations still standing in Woodstock, Chatham and Sarnia.

Niagara Falls contains one of Ontario's oldest stations, and could be the focus of rail excursions to the Falls.

The interior was modest enough, with separate men's and ladies' waiting rooms, and a rounded ticket counter that served both. The decor was wood with wainscotted walls, plaster cornices and cast iron columns. The station also contained rooms for staff, train crews and U.S. Customs officers.

As rail traffic increased, the community of Elgin boomed. Behind the station and along the town's main roads were 20 taverns and hotels. Across the extensive yards stood switchmen's houses, foremen's houses, store houses and a police building. The yards included a roundhouse, repair shop, water tank, coal chutes, and later a YMCA. Eventually Elgin amalgamated with the communities of Clifton and Drummondville to create the City of Niagara Falls.

Although the station still stands, much has changed both about it and around it. Gone now are most of the yard buildings, and much of the yard trackage. A new YMCA is located well to the west. Fewer than a half dozen hotels congregate along the streets, none related to the station. A new bus terminal nearby has made the area a focus for intermodal transport.

While the exterior has been stripped of a dull green paint to reveal the original the red brick, the interior renovations have been less sympathetic. Sadly, the original decor has been covered over with drop ceilings, drywall and linoleum. The railway uses are largely gone now as well, replaced primarily with rental space. And despite the immense draw of the Falls, and the increasing congestion on the area's roads, only four trains call each day. Two are Amtrak's *Maple Leaf* which runs to New York City, and two VIA Rail trains which in effect provide little more than commuter service to and from Toronto.

Because most visitors head for the Falls some distance to the south, or for the shopping malls on the town's perimeter, the commercial core of old Elgin near the station languishes. Even efforts to beautify the streetscape have failed to draw more shoppers. Perhaps more tourist trains, with free shuttle buses to the Falls, would enhance the appeal of the downtown area in this old railway town, with the station again as its focus.

NORTH BAY, CN
Needing Some TLC

To most of Ontario, the City of North Bay is a pleasant city on the shores of a scenic lake, a place where one pauses while venturing further north. While here, one might board the popular cruise vessel the *Chief Commanda*. What is less known about the city is its railway heritage.

After the CPR decided in 1881 to lay out its divisional headquarters by Lake Nipissing, a typical railway grid of streets was laid out

The North Bay station has now lost its tracks, although the building may be restored.

and North Bay was in business. But these were not the only tracks which would enter town. In 1902 the Temiskaming and Northern Ontario Railway (today's Ontario Northland) was built from North Bay as far as New Liskeard. Unlike the CPR, whose vision was transcontinental, the aim of the TNO was to access the vast untapped mining and agricultural resources of Ontario's north east.

Callander stood within a short distance and was the temporary terminus of the Grand Trunk. Although it had reached the shores of Lake Nipissing in 1886, it was not until after its own cross-country line was built through Cochrane far to the north that it too decided to push northward. In 1911 it extended its line into North Bay and from there acquired running rights over the TNO's line to reach Cochrane.

Then in 1914 the determined railway building duo of William Mackenzie and Donald Mann added yet a fourth cross-country line, that being built from Capreol to link with Ottawa and points east. They assigned George Briggs, the CNo's eastern architect, to prepare plans for a station in North Bay. When completed it was used by the GT, the CNo and the TNO. The latter languished without a station of its own until 1994 when it built a multi-modal facility on the southeast end of the city.

The brick station which Briggs created stood at the north east end of the city's commercial core. The CP had already claimed the waterfront 33 years earlier. Because the land sloped sharply upward at this location, the station and the track were well above the level of the streets. In fact, passengers entering from the street side had to climb to the second level to board the trains. An elevator was located in the baggage section.

The use of arches and low rooflines was influenced by the most noted American station builder of that era, H.H. Richardson. The entrance was prominently marked with a high triangular pediment with a porte-cochere beside it leading to a pair of arches. Other passenger entrances were located at track level.

The station was solidly built using red brick on a stone foundation.

The high vaulted waiting room was lit by a chandelier, with smaller chandeliers in the corner bays. Separate smoking rooms for the men and a ladies' room were located on opposite ends of the building, with the ladies enjoying their own direct access to the platform.

Because the CPR had years earlier determined the shape of the town, the arrival of the CNo and its station had little impact. Other than a few essential railway buildings, most of which are gone now, and the physical intrusion of the right of way itself, the townscape was little altered.

In 1986 VIA Rail assumed control of the building and began to "modernize." The high ceiling was covered over and the chandeliers replaced with flourescent lighting.

Just four years later, the federal government under Brian Mulroney removed all rail passenger service from North Bay leaving it to be served by the politically shaky Ontario Northland's trains. Since the Ontario government places such emphasis on roads, even this final rail passenger service is threatened with being sold.

Over the last few years, the station has sat vacant and has been heavily vandalized, trashed by those who seemingly despise their heritage. To add to the dismal scene, the tracks were lifted in the 1990s by the CN as part of their devolution from local railway business. At this writing, however, plans for the building involve the possible sale to a community group which would adapt it to their use, while preserving and enhancing its heritage features.

The building lies on Second Street at the northeast end of Fraser. North Bay's downtown lies between the station and the lake, and contains a beautified main street, while new parklands have opened up the lakeshore between the former CP yards and the water.

Arches, gables and the Canadian Northern logo mark the entrance to the North Bay CN station.

NORTH BAY CP
The Last of the Stone Stations

Nearth Bay is historically one of Ontario's most railway-oriented towns, and its stunning stone station is its centrepiece.

The shores of Lake Nipissing lay in the path of the CPR's new transcontinental scheme, and here the railway put a divisional yard and its regional headquarters. The yards were laid out along the lake, while the town extended in a typical grid-like railway plan behind

The CPR's original North Bay station, left, was still in place even after the new station opened.

them. In fact much of the city owes its origin to the land speculation by John Ferguson who, acting on inside information from his uncle, Douglas McIntyre, was able to acquire the right land in the right place.

While the first two stations were relatively simple two-storey structures, 1902 marked the year when the CPR decided to erect a more elaborate building. As part of its program to provide more pleasing stations, the CPR embarked upon a plan to provide a string of attractive stone stations in the main towns of its Ottawa Valley corridor. In this period such buildings appeared in Pembroke, Arnprior, Renfrew, Almonte and Carleton Place.

Although it was several hundred km from this grouping, North Bay was added to that list. Stones of two hues were hauled from the Arnprior area. While the bulk of the building used large grey stones, the trim was done in reddish stone. In the expansive yards, the roundhouse too was done in stone. The northern section of the station, with its operational and administrative facilities, was two stories in height, while the waiting rooms, on the south end, were but a single storey. The ladies' waiting area, complete with its own fireplace, was unusually large and had separate doors which led both to the street and to the platform. Extensive and prize winning gardens surrounded the station. In the 1940s the entire building was enlarged to become two storeys.

From the platform, trains ran not only east to Ottawa and west to the prairies, but also south to Toronto along the GT tracks. VIA Rail trains called at the station each day until 1990 when the Mulroney government cut all VIA service through the city.

After World War II, the landscape began to change around the stone station. With the conversion from steam to diesel, many of the yard buildings were removed. The district headquarters was pulled out in 1959. The garden became a parking lot and, despite local objections, most of the yard buildings, including the exquisite stone roundhouse, came down. Much of the interior was altered as well, with the waiting area converted to offices. Only the former baggage area remained relatively unscathed.

Following federal designation of the station as a heritage structure, plans began to surface over a re-use, including one for a railway museum. Finally, with the renovation of the North Bay waterfront, the station underwent a nearly half million dollar restoration for use as an education and entertainment centre.

The building remains one of northeastern Ontario's most stunning structures. The only other railway building comparable to it is the TNO's fine stone office building, likewise situated in North Bay.

The yards remain in railway use, and the station continues to dominate its site in the heart of downtown. The building is located on Oak Street at the south end of Fraser.

The stone station built by the CPR is the last in the Ottawa Valley to display that building material.

ORILLIA
No More Trains

$\int$ ince it was designated as a federal heritage railway station, Orillia has lost the single most important feature of its railway landscape, its tracks. Happily, however, it retains most of the other features which train travellers would remember.

Located near the harbour at the foot of King St, the Orillia station marks the junction of several early railway lines including the Northern Railway which was built along the west side of Lake

The tracks are now gone from the front of the Orillia station.

Simcoe in 1869, the Midland Railway which arrived from the east in 1871, and finally, in 1910, the CPR.

At first all three operated separate stations. When the Grand Trunk assumed both the Northern and the Midland in the 1880s, it built a single station to serve both lines. Roads remained quagmires in the area, and the station was located near the water to allow easy transfer onto the steamers plying Lakes Couchiching and Simcoe. This was the case for both freight and passenger traffic.

When World War I broke out in 1914, a military base was established northwest of the town and, to accommodate the added traffic, the GT applied for permission to replace the old depot with a new facility. The plans for the station, drawn up by the railway's own engineers, called for a low building with porte-cocheres on both ends and over the street entrance. The open shelters were to accommodate peak passenger loads from both tourists and soldiers.

Although the overall adornment was minimal, much attention was paid to the little details, such as the eight-sided shingles, the ornate brickwork on the pillars, and the textured stonework around the windows. In a wartime departure from tradition, there was but a single large waiting room with no separate facilities for ladies. Otherwise, the waiting room was amply decorated with five ornamental plaster arches on the side walls. The floor was ofterazo with various coloured marble chips, while the trim was Georgia pine.

A large garden was laid out around the entrance to the station.

The decline in the use of the Orillia station in recent years has been dramatic. As recently as 1971 twelve passenger trains a day called at Orillia. Cuts to rail service by both the provincial government, which ran the *Northlander* to North Bay, and by Brian Mulroney's federal government in 1990, had reduced service to twice a day when VIA Rail's *Canadian* was the only train which still called.

In 1987 the CNR moved out of the building and threatened to demolish it. Pressure by the city saved the station and CN instead leased it to Orillia. Then, a feasibility study, prepared by the Ontario Ministry of Transportation and Communication, laid the groundwork for the station's conversion to a multi-modal transportation and community facility.

As a result of the study and funding from a variety of government programs, since discontinued, the city has saved many of the station's features both inside and out.

In 1997, when CN abandoned its route between Washago and Barrie, the station lost both its trains and its tracks and today functions as a bus depot, Chamber of Commerce and Tourist Information office. Thanks to concerned citizens and councillors, and to meaningful government funding programs, the Orillia station remains an appealing and historic centre of activity for the community.

The building is located on the east side of Front Street at the foot of King Street. Orillia's revitalized waterfront is another block north at the foot of Mississauga Street. Here the former CP station still stands, now converted to a Legion. Here, too, the Ossawippi Restaurant occupies a string of refurbished train coaches located on the former Midland Railway right of way.

OTTAWA
Something New

It may seem odd that a railway station which was built in the same year as Terminal One at Toronto's International Airport would qualify as a "heritage" building. However, the building is considered to be an outstanding example of a grand modern station.

First, its design, which evoked both the historic train shed and the modern airport, was highly regarded at the time. Its most striking element is the vast waiting "room," a covered concourse which visu-

The new Ottawa station was built with cars and buses in mind.

ally combines the modern and the historic. Its high ceiling, laced with dark steel beams, recalls the historic railway train shed, while the circular ticket booth, and the glassed access to the platforms more closely resemble the modern airport. The building's two other physical components, less visible and more functional, are contained within square concrete wings on opposite sides of the concourse.

The glass walls at the two opposite ends of the grand hall open onto the waiting trains to the south, and the waiting vehicles to the north. Lining the concourse are a barber shop, restaurant, first class waiting room, washrooms and lockers. Outside the station, a wide circular landscaped driveway, with special lanes for buses, provides for ease of vehicular access, a concession to the auto age.

The new location was part of a deliberate effort to move train movements away from the heart of the nation's capital, reflecting plans that date back half a century. It was Nicolas Cauchon who in 1922 first suggested creating a belt line around the city, leaving the core free of the noise and smoke which accompanied the early railways. Three decades later, the proposal was acted upon by the city's chief planner Jacques Greber. But it took the approach of Canada's centennial year, and the proposed festivities in Ottawa, to hasten the move. Tracks were removed from the city's core, and a new station constructed. The design of the new station was the work of J. Parkin and Associates, a firm which had gained a wide reputation for its cutting edge international style buildings, including Toronto Airport's Terminal One.

Ottawa has gone through a succession of stations, ranging from the simple wooden shed of the Prescott and Bytown Railway of the 1850s, to the chateauesque CPR station in the 1890s and the still standing, but inaccessible, classic revival union station on Rideau Street opposite the Chateau Laurier Hotel. It was fitting, therefore, that a country which was built on railways should have as a centennial project yet another grand railway station.

It is somewhat ironic that while the Ottawa station is being celebrated as a heritage building, Toronto Airport's Terminal One, its contemporary, is vilified as begin crowded and outdated and faces demolition.

Ottawa's station is located on Alta Vista Blvd, south of the Queensway (Highway 417) and offers ten trains daily to and from Montreal and Toronto.

The interior of the Ottawa station earned it many accolades and restored to Ontario the notion of the grand station.

OWEN SOUND
The CPR's Bold New Design

Low, flat and streamlined, the Owen Sound CPR station represented a radical departure in railway station design.

Following World War II and the sharp peak in rail passenger traffic that occurred during it, the railways set out to recapture their passenger business. Cars and superhighways had yet to overtake the landscape and the culture. To draw travellers back to the trains, the CPR purchased a quantity of comfortable new coaches, and replaced

The station at Owen Sound, now trackless, reflects the CPR's modernistic station style.

many of its stations with modern new streamlined facilities.

Built in a design known to architects as the "international style," these buildings had their roots in the art deco era of geometric shapes and curved surfaces. One storey in height, the Owen Sound station boasted a curved wrap-around canopy and metallic silhouette letters atop the roof. Windows were large, and in one instance wrapped around as well. The walls were mottled brick set on Indiana limestone and, although only 15 feet (5m) high, the building measured more than 130 feet (26m) long.

The station interior consisted of the waiting room which looked out over the harbour on the west side, and was trimmed with birch plywood panelling and stained walnut while the waiting room floors were red quarry tile. Even the furniture was modernistic with green leather and chrome legs. The ticket window was designed with white alloy metal and glass brick. The remaining rooms included the freight office, baggage area and agent's facilities.

Located on the harbour, the station represented the CPR's historical connection to Georgian Bay. In 1884 the Toronto Grey and Bruce opened the line to provide western grain shippers with easy access to ocean ports. The first station was a low, wide board and batten building with extensive yards and a roundhouse located a short distance to the north. In 1911 a disastrous fire destroyed the grain elevators and the CPR moved its grain shipments to a new port several km east named Port McNicoll. Owen Sound nevertheless continued to be an important port.

A rival station had been built on the opposite side of the harbour by the CN, and the two buildings faced each other across the water.

The station represented an experimental design which was being repeated at other locations in Ontario. In the south, which was well represented by solid existing stations, new stations were built to this style at Leaside and Pendleton, while in northern Ontario they appeared primarily in newly planned resource towns such as Spanish, Heron Bay, Marathon, Terrace Bay and Red Rock. The new station attached to the communications building in White River followed this pattern as well. Only those at White River and Spanish survive.

The CN followed suit with "international" stations at Midland, that railway's first, at Pembroke Junction, and on the new trackage along the St Lawrence where the seaway had flooded the earlier route. These appeared at Cornwall, Morrisburg, Iroquois, Long Sault and Ingleside.

By 1970, however, the experiment had failed. Cars and trucks were winning the day, and the CPR gave up on rail passenger service entirely. Freight service was halted to Owen Sound in the early 1990s and the rails of the historic line were lifted soon after that.

Owen Sound's downtown, while not far from the station, is neither functionally nor visually connected with it. In fact, all railway structures are gone, and most of the land in the immediate vicinity of the trackless station is either waste land, or parking lots.

Much work has gone into converting the industrial harbour into a pedestrian area, with walkways and gardens along the water, and benches from which to watch the freighters glide into the port. On the opposite shore of the harbour, the CN station still stands and is now a marine museum and information centre. The CPR station is located on 1st Avenue a few blocks north of the intersection of 10th Street and 3rd Ave, which is the downtown core.

PARRY SOUND
The Witch's Hat

The first thing one notices about the CPR's wooden Parry Sound railway station is the unusual conical roof above the waiting room. Nicknamed the "witch's hat," it was a feature which railway companies thought would attract passengers. This is especially true of the line the railway built in 1906 to link Toronto with its main line at a junction near Sudbury.

Because two new rivals, the Canadian Northern Railway and the Grand Trunk Pacific, were on the verge of cutting into the CPR's near

Following its heritage designation, the Parry Sound CPR station became an art gallery.

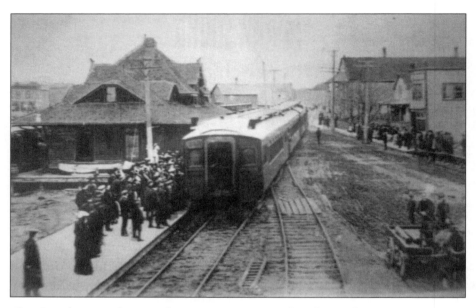

The Canadian Northern Railway gave Parry Sound its first railway station.

monopoly on the prairies, the CP thought it only right that it should likewise absorb a share of the Ontario market which its rivals had had to themselves. This 260 mile (350 km) line would bring the Toronto market directly onto their main line.

But the CPR also had their eye on the rapidly growing tourism market. Already expert at promoting the Rockies, Lake of the Woods and St Andrews by the Sea in New Brunswick as destinations, the railway turned its attention to the lakelands of Muskoka and Parry Sound. Because there was little local freight, the railway built its stations in such a style and in such locations so as to attract tourists. Stations at Bala and Lake Joseph led directly to steamer connections, while special railway lodges were built at the French River.

With its access to the Thirty Thousand Islands, Parry Sound was promoted as a key tourist destination. And the station style reflected that emphasis. The tower over the waiting room gave the station an almost "castle-like" grandeur, especially when viewed from below. From the tower itself, passengers enjoyed a modest vista of the town and the rocky woodlands upon which the town was built. The circular waiting room measured 24 feet (36m) in diameter, and boasted curved benches along the windows, and exposed beams. A separate waiting room was set aside for the ladies. Although the original wood work was later covered over both inside and out, it did remain in place.

Because Parry Sound's urban form was already established before the CPR arrived, the location of the station did not affect the town's growth. Although close to the town's core, it was not part of it, as the track circled around the town on a high rocky ridge. The high level bridge upon which the tracks crossed the harbour is the highest railway bridge east of the Rockies. Nor did the railway significantly impact its immediate surroundings. No hotels, warehouses, cattle pens or factories appeared near the station. The only other structures were a baggage shed and water tower and both are now gone, as is the station garden.

VIA Rail continued to call until 1990 when the Mulroney government forced it onto the nearby CN tracks. CP used the building only for another two years before leasing it to the town. Following years of uncertainty, and even a bit of local opposition, the station has now been restored and was opened in 2001 as an art gallery, with the rotunda available for gatherings and events.

The station is located on Avenue Rd, just east of Waubeek St.

The town's other station, built by the CNR, is located on Church Street several blocks east of downtown, and now houses the Chamber of Commerce as well as a VIA Rail waiting area.

Located amid the spectacular scenery of the Thirty Thousand Islands, Parry Sound hosts coastal boat cruises and a summer music festival known as the Festival of the Sound. Amid its many other attractions, Parry Sound's railway legacy will not be forgotten.

PORT HOPE
Canada's Oldest Station

Port Hope is one of Ontario's great heritage success stories. Here is a town which has retained its 19th century streetscapes almost intact. And the survival of its 1856 Grand Trunk railway station is part of that story.

Port Hope's growth began in the 1830s with the dredging of its harbour. The Ganaraska River, which flows down from the hills to the north had long attracted mills to its water power, but the improvements to the river mouth meant more shipping.

The little stone station at Port Hope is said to be Canada's oldest station to remain in continuous railway use.

When the railway craze arrived a decade or so later, Port Hope vied with its nearby rival, Cobourg, over which town would first gain a rail link to the timber and grain of the hinterland. Cobourg won initially with its Cobourg Peterborough and Chemong Lake Railway. However, with the closing of its doomed trestle across Rice Lake, Port Hope gained ascendency with what would become the Midland Railway.

The arrival of the Grand Trunk Railway with its vital Montreal to Toronto route brought economic prosperity to the towns through which it passed. And in 1856 Port Hope acquired its charming stone station. Unlike most other GT station sites, that in Port Hope was in fact close to the lake. To cross the wide harbour, the GT constructed a long stone trestle, then to access the wharf, added a series of spur lines. Meanwhile, the roundhouse, station and yards of the Midland Railway were all located beneath and to the north of the trestle.

While it was never a divisional point, the yards at Port Hope contained an agent's house and two section dwellings, as well as a repair shop, carpenter's shop, stock yard and freight shed. The station itself was divided into a waiting room on the east, agent's office in the middle and baggage area on the west. Later, when a separate baggage shed was built, the west section became a ladies' waiting area.

The station style was identical to that being built at 34 other locations on the Toronto Montreal line, being a low stone building with wide eaves and the trademark French doors along the sides, six in the case of Port Hope. Two such openings were located at the ends with a circular vent in the gable immediately above. Like most others, the doors were filled in to create windows, while the central portion was boxed in to become the site of the operator's bay.

Port Hope went on to add three other stations, the Midland, where the parking lot of a grocery store now sprawls, the Canadian Pacific, situated east of the river on Peter Street and now demolished, and the Canadian Northern, now a government office on Ontario Street.

With the building of the highways, Port Hope ceased to be a railway town. The wharf trackage was lifted, and the yard trackage and buildings removed, while the lines of the Midland and the Canadian

Northern railways were abandoned entirely. The CP station was demolished in the late 1970s. In the early 1980s when the same fate appeared to await the Grand Trunk stone station, the citizens of Port Hope decided that wasn't going to happen.

In a remarkable display of cooperation, the CN, VIA Rail, the Ontario Heritage Foundation and the Ontario Ministry of Citizenship and Culture, along the local Architectural Conservancy, joined forces to raise funds and restore the deteriorating stone facade. The waiting room was restored to its 1890s appearance, complete with paint scheme, wooden benches and period light fixtures. VIA Rail's morning and evening trains serve the town's commuter market.

Although it stands alone now, with the lake as a backdrop and overgrown trackless yards in front, the station in Port Hope retains the appearance and atmosphere of its legacy. It is, many claim, the oldest station in Canada to have remained in continuous railway use.

And that fits right in with the rest of the town. Besides the station, Port Hope has preserved two major residential neighbourhoods, one which predates the railway, the other which developed as a result of

the railway, its old port area with a series of ships' captain's homes, a restored theatre, and one of the best examples of a 19th century main street to be found anywhere in Ontario.

The station is situated on Choate Street west of John. In addition to the morning and evening commuter trains, there is also both a mid-day and midnight service. Despite the few stops, the station is excellent for train watching, with the historic trestle nearby, and the CP main line visible a sort distance to the north.

When the Port Hope station was restored, the waiting room was returned to its 19th-century appearance.

PRESCOTT
Surrounded by History

Despite the fact that the GTR station in Prescott is the largest of the original old stone stations to survive on that historic line, it represents little more than a footnote in Prescott's rich history and heritage.

Prescott owes its origin to the rapids on the St Lawrence River which foamed past its piers. At this point people and goods, bound from Lake Ontario to Montreal, disembarked from the steamships to bypass the terrible cataracts which plagued the river. The town was

The Prescott station is largely forgotten thanks to the town's many other historic features.

founded in 1810 and named for Robert Prescott, Governor-in-Chief for all Canada. By the 1840s it could claim 18 hotels and taverns.

Because of its strategic importance, a railway line was built to link it with Bytown on the Ottawa River in 1850. In 1855 the Montreal to Brockville section of the Grand Trunk railway was finished and at Prescott the railway built a stone wayside station using the largest of its standard plans. Squat and single storied, it was constructed of stone and distinguished by its low pitched roof and stone chimneys at each of the four corners. Although similar to those at Port Hope and St Mary's, the size classification was determined by the number of arched French doors along the side, and that at Prescott could boast seven.

As was its custom, the GTR also located the building well outside of town and at some distance from the wharves. This allowed the railway to snub competing water-borne shippers and also, it is said, to allow its supporters to more easily speculate in those lands for which the stations were proposed.

The area around the Prescott station acquired a large freight shed which measured 37 by 121 feet (12 by 40 m), a separate frame baggage room, a coal shed, a section house and stockyard. Behind the building a boarding house for train crew was later added. Although Prescott was never designated as a divisional point, it did contain sidings and sorting yards, and the station was once advertized as having a restaurant.

The Prescott station consisted of three components, the waiting room, the operational and ticketing area, and what was possibly a restaurant area, as there was a separate baggage shed. Over the years, the French doors were partially filled in, and an operator's bay added to the track side of the building.

Gradually Prescott's urban boundary grew out to the station with residential development to the south and industrial growth to the east along the tracks. Further east, where the GT crossed the PB, later the CPR, a small railway village known as Prescott Junction developed.

Even though the railway was confined to a relatively small chapter in Prescott's history, its position has diminished even further. Most of the yard buildings are gone, the village at the junction has vanished, as has the CP line to the river. Finally, in 2001, VIA Rail discontinued its two daily trains, effectively ending Prescott's active railway heritage.

Prescott's railway heritage has always remained on its periphery. A visit to the river bank leads to the early buildings such as taverns, houses, churches and commercial buildings, all of which relate to the history of shipping on the river. Fort Wellington, a restored 1830s fort, is situated on the eastern edge of the village. Heritage walking tours list the station simply under "other points of interest."

The building lies largely forgotten at the north end of St Lawrence Street at the corner of Railway Ave.

SARNIA
Joseph Hobson's Finest Hour

Perhaps one of the most striking railway stations in Ontario is the Tunnel Station at Sarnia.

Sarnia was at one point the terminus for no fewer than three railway lines. In 1859 the Grand Trunk completed its line from a junction just north of St Mary's to nearby Point Edward. The Great Western constructed its route parallel to, but south of, that of the Grand Trunk with a terminal by the wharf in Sarnia, while the Erie and Huron was extended from Lake Erie to the south end of Sarnia in 1873.

The Tunnel Station at Sarnia is one of Ontario's most attractive.

Meanwhile, on the opposite bank of the St Clair River, the American lines were collecting in Port Huron. Prior to the 1880s, ferries shuttled back and forth across the river carrying the rail cars between termini. Then, following the absorption of the GW by the GT, Joseph Hickson, the GT's general manager, boldly suggested a railway tunnel be built under the river to speed up shipping.

When it opened in September 1891, it could claim to be the world's longest and largest underwater train tunnel and the first such international facility.

Because all passengers and freight would now be heading straight through the tunnel, and bypassing Sarnia's wharf station, a new station was needed. Joseph Hobson, the former GW architect and veteran station designer, was called upon and created what is considered to be one of his finest stations.

Using his trademark steep hip gables, Hobson designed a long narrow building with distinctive Flemish gables at each end, while above the central section soared a much higher, two-storey hip gable. Considered one of Canada's most creative station architects of the era, Hobson also designed stations at Chatham, Woodstock, Allandale and Guelph.

The location of the Tunnel Station had a significant impact upon Sarnia's growth. With the new facility as well as major new yards more than 2 km from the old town centre, workers' homes began to gather around the station grounds. A wooden immigration shed, bunkhouse, and the "largest roundhouse on the system" were also built nearby. In an attempt to tie the building into the old downtown, a series of parks was created from the station to the waterfront and then to the centre of town.

Eventually, the town grew to meet the station, and the area is now a part of Sarnia's urban area. Meanwhile, Point Edward, which before the tunnel was the more important of the two communities, now retains nothing of its railway heritage, save a display steam engine near the Bluewater Bridge to the U.S.

After acquiring the building, VIA Rail gutted and modernized the interior, leaving very little of its original decor intact. The dull grey paint which covered the original two-tone paintwork has been removed to reveal the natural bricks. As part of the renovation, the local community has come together to celebrate the heritage of Hobson's fine creation and at the west platform in a small garden a brass plaque was unveiled to commemorate the railway tunnel.

In contrast to the trend at most of Ontario's historic railway facilities, activity at Sarnia has been increasing. The Sarnia yard was designated as one of CN's five major yards across Canada. With the opening of a new and larger St Clair River tunnel in the late 1990s, container cars and double decker passenger coaches can now pass easily beneath the water. Only four passenger trains, however, call daily at the station.

The station lies a block south of Campbell Street between Indian Rd and Vidal St, two of the city's major thoroughfares. The entrance to the tunnel lies beside Andrew Street west of Vidal. Sarnia has another station. Considerably less appealing and not designated by the Station Act, the CSX freight depot lies at the end of Clifford Street west of Vidal.

SCHREIBER
On Superior's Shore

For those who know Schreiber, it may seem like little more than a line of motels and gas stations along the Trans Canada Highway's scenic Lake Superior route. However, a short journey down its side streets will lead to the large railway station and a glimpse into the town's railway legacy.

The rugged and isolated nature of the land through which the CPR was building its transcontinental line in the 1880s meant that supplies needed to arrive by boat. One of the five landing points for the men, equipment and supplies was known as Isbester Landing.

Although less important now, the station at Schreiber is still the focus of the busy railway town.

Then, thanks to its position halfway between White River and Thunder Bay, the location was designated as a divisional point as well. Here, three km inland from the landing, the CPR laid out extensive yards with the usual railway buildings such as roundhouse, coal docks, repair shops, and a station large enough to accommodate offices, operations and passengers.

The CPR laid out the town on both sides of the track, with the executives occupying larger homes south of the station, the workers to the north. The town was named after Collingwood Schreiber, a prominent 19th century railway executive A railway YMCA also stood near the station, but was removed following the closing of the railway YMCA program. As with most CPR stations, the grounds contained attractive gardens.

In the 1920s fire destroyed the station, which was the second on this location, as well as the original roundhouse. A new 20-stall roundhouse was built, along with a larger station. The 1920s, however, was not an era of large scale station building. While a few grand stations were indeed being added to major cities like Hamilton and Halifax, smaller communities, and divisional points in particular were getting structures which were much simpler in appearance and more functional in layout.

Such was the case in Schreiber. The new facility was a straight forward two storey affair, constructed of brick, with very little in the way of exterior architectural embellishments.

Inside, a waiting room occupied the central portion, part of which was set aside for ladies. At the east end was a large restaurant, typical of divisional stations, while at the west end were the offices of the agent and the operator as well as express and baggage facilities. The second floor contained the divisional responsibilities such as offices, drafting room and meeting room.

During the 1950s the face of railroading changed fundamentally and irreversibly. With diesel, divisional points were not needed at the same intervals, and many of Schreiber's functions were transferred to Chapleau. Then, in the 1960s, its traffic control functions were relocated to Toronto. In 1988 its status was further downgraded from divisional headquarters to simple divisional point with regional responsibilities. It did, however, continue to function as an administrative centre and as a terminal for train crews.

The completion of the Trans Canada Highway in the late 1960s helped to draw the town away from its dependency on the declining railway operations, as motels, gas stations, and restaurants appeared along the new road.

Then, in 1992, passenger service was eliminated as VIA Rail's popular *Canadian* was relocated from the CPR's scenic Lake Superior route to the more inland route of the CNR. The waiting room was then converted to office space, and an era ended.

To travellers on the Trans Canada Highway, Schreiber's railway legacy is not apparent. One must leave the highway and drive to the centre of town to see the now quiet yards and the large station. Here, too, are the neat railway homes which still line the streets on the two sides of the tracks.

The original station at Schreiber quickly proved to be too small for the expanding facilities.

SEARCHMONT
In the Mountains of Algoma

If the attractive Searchmont station looks right at home in its mountain setting, it is because railway builder Francis Clergue wanted it that way. Located in the Algoma mountain country 90 km north of Sault Ste Marie, Searchmont was to have been a railway junction and a resort, with a station designed to match.

Clergue's first grand plan to build a railway from Lake Huron to

The grand style of the Searchmont station reflects the original plans to make the place into a busy resort and railway junction.

Hudson's Bay changed dramatically when he discovered vast deposits of iron on the way. Suddenly, the line changed from one which would ship fish to the US to one which would haul iron ore to the smokey smelters in Sault Ste Marie. And so the Algoma Central Railway was born.

The Searchmont station is busy in the summer with canoers and campers.

By 1902 both the Grand Trunk and Canadian Pacific Railways were heavily promoting the tourist potential of their lines. The CP enjoyed the benefit of having the Rocky Mountains right on its route, while the Grand Trunk had recently acquired a railway into Algonquin Park. Rail tours were rapidly becoming the vacation of choice for the elite of North America.

In that year Clergue purchased a boat, the *King Edward*, which would carry passengers from places like Detroit and Goderich north to Sault Ste Marie where they would board Clergue's trains to experience the stunning beauty of the Agawa Canyon and the mountains of Algoma.

At Goulais, the name of the planned junction of the Algoma Central with the Algoma Eastern Railway, Clergue proposed to build a grand hotel. A new community was developed in the area with a saw and shingle mill and a charcoal kiln. Meanwhile 145 families of pioneers were induced to settle the land around it. Clergue instructed his Master of Works, W.Z. Earle, to design a grand station for this location.

The result was a two-storey station with a freight shed on the north end, a rounded waiting room on the south end, and the agent's quarters upstairs. The effect of the waiting room roof was that of a low tower, then the rage with station builders across the continent. In 1902 the 30' by 100' (9m by 30m) station was completed at a cost of $5,000 (or about $500,000 today). About the same time, the name of both the community and the station were changed to honour T.C. Search, treasurer of the Lake Superior Consolidated Mine.

But things did not pan out for Clergue. The following year his companies had folded. The industries at Searchmont shut down, and most of the farmers moved away. The projected route of the Algoma Eastern Railway was scrapped, and the hoped-for junction never materialized. Although the town retained a store and railway hotel, its population had plummeted to fifty. But it still had its grand station.

Following World War II the fortunes of Searchmont picked up. A road was built into the remote valley and tourists began to arrive. Skiing became popular and the ACR initiated ski trains. Tour trains began carrying passengers to the Agawa Canyon while local trains boarded cottagers and canoers at the Searchmont station.

Sadly, the circular waiting room had been destroyed by fire in 1929, but the overall impression remained that of a grand station. Little has changed on the inside. Three walls of the waiting room and the agent's office all retain their wooden walls and wainscotting.

The station has been closed now for several years, and despite its heritage designation, and local efforts to save it, its future is in doubt.

OBA

The grand towered station at Oba can easily be categorized as a ghost station in a ghost town. Although located at the junction of the Algoma Central Railway and the Canadian National, the Oba station was designed by R.B. Pratt of the Canadian Northern Railway and built in 1913. Two storeys in height and constructed in wood, the station sported a decorative tower on one corner of the building closely resembling the original Canadian Northern station in Fort Frances.

Although Oba was not a divisional point for either railway, it did include repair shops and crew accommodation. Being an isolated community (which it still is), the railway was the little community's *raison d'etre*.

The main level of the station was used for passengers, freight and train operations, and the second floor was reserved for the agent and his family.

With the switch by the railways from steam to diesel, the facilities at Oba were closed, and most of the village was abandoned. The empty building still stands and provides crude shelter for passengers traveling by rail to and from the local fish and hunt camps. Both VIA Rail and the ACR still stop here, VIA by request, the ACR by schedule. Sadly, the vacant building is heavily vandalized and has suffered much damage from the weather.

Although it was not designated under the HRSPA, the Oba station is the only original station built by the Canadian Northern Railway to survive between Thunder Bay and North Bay. And it, like the town which stood around it, is likely to disappear.

Oba lies about 80 km south of Hearst on the ACR and is accessible only by rail or by logging roads.

The towered Oba station before it was closed and vandalized.

SIOUX LOOKOUT
The Tudor Look

Located right on the main street, the CN station in Sioux Lookout Ontario is the town's most imposing structure. This two-storied stucco station is decidedly different from the other divisional stations on this remote northern line. If the twin cross gables at the station's two ends don't draw the eye, then the attractive Tudor Revival half timber woodwork decidedly does.

Sioux Lookout was planned as one of a string of divisional towns spaced at roughly 180 km intervals across remote northern Ontario.

The Tudor style on the Sioux Lookout station makes it distinct among Ontario stations.

This was part of Wilfred Laurier's scheme for a third transcontinental line to connect Quebec City with Prince Rupert and provide prairie grain growers with a direct rail link to ice-free ocean ports.

Other divisional towns from east to west included Cochrane, Hearst, Armstrong, Nakina and Redditt. All were utterly isolated and totally dependent upon the railway for their links to the outside, both social and economic. Of these, Cochrane and Nakina have retained their stations in good order. The station at Armstrong is vacant and vandalized, while the identical stations at Hearst and Redditt were demolished.

Although Sioux Lookout grew around the station, with the usual grid pattern of streets, it was not railway owned, as was the CPR town of White River, for example. The main street passed by the back of the station, while a handsome brick YMCA building stood a little to the west.

Being in a divisional point, the yards included a roundhouse, water tower, coal docks, express building, and a section house. During the 1960s, after CN switched from coal to diesel and downgraded the status of the yards, these features were all removed. Even the YMCA, arguably for many years the grandest building in the town, was torn down in 1990, despite local objections.

The station featured the usual array of rooms: separate general and ladies' waiting rooms, operating and agent facilities, and that fixture at most divisional stations, a restaurant. Eleven offices filled out the second floor. But with the removal of most of those divisional functions, the offices were closed. Cutbacks to passenger service reduced the size of the waiting room and closed the agent's office, while the restaurant was converted to locker rooms. Upstairs, the office now sat silent and unheated, while the basement filled with water. Private restoration is currently being proposed.

Passenger service now consists only of VIA Rail's thrice weekly *Canadian*, which carries not only cross country travellers, but many who are bound for lakeside cottages and camps, and the many remote native villages which still lack road access.

While a number of residents are still employed by the railway, mainly as crew or maintenance workers, the town has lost its dependence on the trains. When the new highway 72 opened in the late 1960s, Sioux Lookout was suddenly linked to the outside by car. The town also prospers from the many hunting and fishing lodges which draw outdoor enthusiasts to the clear air and the silent lakes in the area. Thanks to its airport, the town functions as the main service and administration centre for northwestern Ontario's many remote First Nations communities.

While Sioux Lookout may have lost most of its links with the railway, the location and appearance of its station won't let the town forget its legacy entirely.

VIA's *Canadian* makes its scheduled stop at the Sioux Lookout station.

ST CATHARINES
the Fruit Station

It's confusing enough for first-time visitors to find their way around St Catharines' streets without trying to locate its station. The town developed as a mill town in the 1780s and grew along a network of pioneer trails. Early roads approached it from different angles, resulting in an urban pattern that is anything but straight forward.

Then, when the Great Western Railway arrived in 1853, it built its line and its station on the south side of Twelve Mile Creek, then the route of the Welland Canal, opposite to where the town stood. The station did, however, offer convenient access to the canal. While interaction between the canal and the railway tapered off, the construction of the Burgoyne Street bridge over the river valley and the

The current station in St Catharines is used largely by commuters.

inauguration of trolley service to the station in 1914 made the railway much more convenient to the town's residents. In fact it reduced travelling time from downtown to a mere three minutes, a time unmatched even today.

The first station was the usual long, low, wooden station used by the railway for its small town locations. Today's station is the third to occupy the site and was built by the Grand Trunk in 1917. For railway station architecture it marked a period of transition from the large fanciful stations which bespoke more optimistic times, to the smaller and simpler designs which reflected the reality of stagnating or even declining railway fortunes.

The single storey structure could claim few embellishments other than an attractive rounded gable above the operator's bay window. A large port-cochere extended out along the platform at the east end of the building, while a separate freight building stood at a distance to the west.

Despite its distance from the town, industry was soon attracted to the station site. Welch's Grape Juice built a factory, while Jordan's added a winery. At the time, the Niagara region was quickly becoming a major tender fruit area and speedy transportation provided by the railways augmented the importance of St Catharines' station.

With the building of the QEW, and the growth in truck haulage, all that has changed. No longer do freights haul fruit or factory products from the station. The station itself has changed as well. The interior, simple enough to begin with, was altered with a new drop ceiling, masonite walls, and linoleum over the wooden floor. The space between the passenger and freight buildings has been infilled to accommodate commercial tenants while the operator's bay is now a doorway to the tracks. What was once the station garden is now a parking lot.

Despite the loss of freight activity, the lot is usually filled with the cars of commuters who use the early morning VIA train to Toronto. The station is also a stop for Amtrak's New York bound *Maple Leaf*.

The station sits at the corner of Permilla St, the former main access to the site, and Great Western Ave, a name that bespeaks the early railway heritage of the area.

ST MARY'S JUNCTION
Diamond in the Rough

What is arguably Ontario's most significant small scale station, comes as a surprise. The first surprise is the location of the St Mary's Junction station. Rather than being anywhere near the town, it was built on a parcel of land more than two km away. The second surprise involves its simple style, basically a stone rectangle with an unembellished low pitched roof. And the third, disheartening, element, is the neglect which it continues to suffer.

In the 1850s the main western route of the Grand Trunk Railway followed a line between Stratford and Sarnia. However, a branch to the growing district capital of London and its link with the Great Western Railway was deemed crucial.

While the junction point would be St Mary's, a growing mill town

The neglected Grand Trunk station at St Mary's Junction is the only original station from that era to have remained unaltered.

on the North Thames River, the site selected for the station was nowhere near where the town's proponents wanted it. In fact it was a full two km north of the town. The land, as it turns out, was a parcel owned by none other than the mayor of the City of London whom the railway was courting to obtain running rights into his city.

The GT used the same station plan in many locations on both its eastern and western section. This was a square plan, with arched French doors on the sides and ends and originated in England with the GT's British Chief Architect, Francis Thomson, who had designed many similar structures on the North Midland and Chester and Holyhead Railways. A number of other railway buildings appeared at the junction, including a small stone roundhouse, yards and agent's house.

Located at a critical junction point, the station was vital in coordinating traffic along the busy lines which met here and was staffed day and night by telegraph operators. In 1863 a telegraph operator from the Stratford Junction station was assigned night duties at the station. An inventor in his spare time, the young man devised a mechanism which would automatically send a mandatory night time electronic signal to the dispatcher in Stratford each half hour while he, against the rules, slept. One fateful night, a train passed the sleeping operator, and was prevented from crashing into another only by an alert agent down the line. The operator was hauled onto the carpet and, as the story goes, threatened with arrest. He then hastily returned to his native Michigan where he switched to full time inventing. His name was Thomas Alva Edison. His desk from that station is now on display at the Edison Institute.

The station layout was, as with the others in this style, divided into a waiting area, baggage area, and agent's area. But unlike the eastern section of the Grand Trunk, where eight such stations survive, that at St Mary's Junction is the only original GT station on the western section to remain standing. Other similar stations at Stratford, Guelph and Kitchener were all replaced during the railway's upgrading phase between 1895 and 1910.

The people of St Mary's were unhappy at having to travel so far to their station when the tracks ran right through town. Finally, in 1907, an attractive brick station was built by the main street and serves train travellers to this day. Meanwhile, out at the junction, things are quiet. The former main line to Sarnia is now gone, the yards covered over by a junk yard, and all railway buildings have been removed.

While the junction station remained in railway use until the 1970s, its exterior was virtually untouched, and it remains the only original GT station whose full length French doors were never filled in to create windows, nor was an operator's bay window ever installed.

It is disappointing, therefore, that despite a National Historic Sites and Monuments Board plaque, and designation under the HRSPA, it remains unattended and surrounded by a high chain link fence to prevent the usual vandalism which so often plagues such abandoned sites.

Ironically, the newer downtown station, while not federally designated, has been preserved and restored. In 1988 the Town of St Mary's purchased the attractive building and moved its parks and recreation department into it, while fixing up the VIA ticketing area to resemble its historic appearance. This station is a single storey brick structure with sweeping bell cast roof and a semi-conical gable over the rounded bay window. The four daily trains which call at the downtown station, pass the junction station with hardly a second glance.

The junction station is on Glass Street east of County Road 19 (James Street). The active station is located near the intersection of Queen Street and James.

An early view of the downtown station in St Mary's.

ST THOMAS
The Longest Station

One of the first federally designated heritage stations in Ontario, St Thomas's Canada Southern station just seems to go on and on. And on. While only 36 feet (12 m) wide, it stretches along the track for an incredible 354 feet (120 m).

Canada Southern, the first major American line to build across southern Ontario, was clearly making a statement with the grandeur of its station. Before 1850 St Thomas was a thriving community on the banks of Kettle Creek. It had been the heart of an extensive colony created by Thomas Talbot who had been given a massive land

The remarkable Italianate station at St Thomas is the longest small town station in Ontario.

grant along Lake Erie's north shore. To honour this colonizer, the community named itself St. Thomas. Contemporary accounts of his intemperate attitude to some prospective settlers dispute the "saint" part of the name, however.

In 1854 southwestern Ontario's first railway line, the Great Western, opted for a route well to the north of St Thomas, passing instead through a community called London. As a result, the latter boomed, attracting industries and factories to its rails.

Then, following the American civil war, American railway promoters began looking to southwestern Ontario as a short cut between Detroit and Buffalo. In 1870 the citizens of St Thomas voted to grant the CS $25,000 if it would locate its headquarters there. Suddenly concerned about having a rival in the area, the Great Western began building a branch line from London to St Thomas. The Great Western arrived in February 1872; the Canada Southern followed six months later. Within a few decades, St Thomas would have no fewer than seven railway lines, three of which used the CS station.

To underscore its dominance, the Canada Southern built a remarkable station that remains unique in Canada. Although American, it was designed by an Ontario land surveyor turned architect named Edgar Berryman. To emphasize its distinctiveness, he adopted an Italianate style for the building, a style popular in the early years of the 19th century, but seldom used for railway stations. In fact, no other station in Canada was anything like it.

Two storeys high, it used 400,000 light red bricks. There were 44 rows of windows and eight chimneys protruding from the roof. The windows were tall and graceful, and topped with arches. At the two ends, four stylized pillars appeared to support the triangular gable, giving it the aspect of a Roman temple. Two open passageways cut through the building. The entire structure was surrounded by a flat roofed canopy supported by iron pillars.

Inside, on the ground floor, were a dining room with a 20-foot ceiling located near the east end of the building, while on the west end were separate men's and ladies' waiting rooms. All ground floor rooms had access to both the tracks and the town. On the second floor a long corridor connected the offices of the General Superintendent, paymaster, solicitor, freight agents and quarters for servants and waitresses.

In front of the station stretched the railway's extensive yards, beyond which lay the various engine and repair shops. On the town side of the station were a landscaped park and a railway YMCA. The CS station was one which significantly shaped St Thomas's urban form. While the original townsite lay along the banks of Kettle Creek 2km to the west, where many early buildings still stand, the railway added their facilities well to the east. Here grew a village of workers' homes, industries, cafes and hotels. Soon the two villages grew together giving the town the linear appearance of today.

By 1968 the Canada Southern had become part of the ill-fated Penn Central empire which went bankrupt in 1976. After a brief ownership under Conrail, the line was acquired jointly by CN and CP, and now is solely a CN line.

With the yards and shops no longer needed, most of St Thomas's railway operations were shut down. The yards are overgrown, while the rails see only an occasional short-line freight. The shops, however, have become part of the popular Elgin Railway Museum.

Despite its long period of inactivity, it appears that the station will also survive. After years of controversy and debate (including the proposal by one developer to sell the station's bricks) the elegant building is now being redeveloped as a nursing residence. Sadly, although the YMCA building still stands, the former station gardens have been paved for a parking lot for a tediously ordinary commercial development.

Regrettably, all other stations in St Thomas have been demolished, along with nearly every rural station which lined the railway. The longest station in small town Ontario stands on the south side of Talbot Street, the town's main street, between First and Ross Streets. The railway museum is accessed from Wellington Street.

STRATFORD
The Bard's Gateway

It is most fitting that one of Ontario's most park-like towns would possess one of its most park-like stations. Unlike nearly every other surviving station in Ontario, most of which once claimed gardens, the Stratford station retains its lovely landscaped lawns.

It was almost a fluke that led to the town's current status as a leading Shakespearean venue. When the Canada Company was building its settlement road to Goderich on Lake Huron, it crossed a small

Although shorn now of its tower, the large station at Stratford remains a handsome structure as befits this Shakespeare-loving town.

A steam era view of the Stratford station before the tower was removed. Note the platform lamp standards.

river which it called initially the Little Thames. A few settlers lingered here, one of whom opened a tavern called the Shakespeare Inn after his favourite playwright. After he was given a portrait of Shakespeare, the place became known as Stratford.

Prior to 1850 it was a swampy mill hamlet with a population of fewer than 200. Then, when the new county of Perth was created, it became the county seat. As such, it would certainly warrant a station on the proposed Grand Trunk Railway. In 1856 a small station was erected well away from the town's core. About the same time another railway line was on its way, the Buffalo Brantford and Goderich being built to link the American markets via Fort Erie with the Lake Huron port of Goderich. The two lines crossed in Stratford, and the station became known as Stratford Junction.

In 1871 the GTR, now owner of both lines, chose Stratford as a divisional point and replaced its earlier depot with a larger structure. Lured by a $120,000 bonus from the town, the GT created one of Ontario's largest railway towns with a roundhouse, repair shops and engine shops. By 1901 Stratford's population topped 10,000, 80% of whom depended upon the GT shops for their livelihood.

Then in 1911, threatened with the incursion of the rival Canadian Pacific and Canadian Northern railways, the Grand Trunk replaced the deteriorating old wooden station with one of its grandest, and one of its last, stations. Spurning a call for a union station to be shared among the three rivals, the GT's president, Charles M Hayes, built a massive two-storey stone station, dominated by a 60-foot tall battlemented tower.

The tower rose above the entrance on the street side, while above the bay on the track side the effect was balanced by a large gable. The building, one of the GT's largest, measured 60 feet by 151 feet (18m by 46m). The main lobby was large and central, with the ticket office directly opposite the entrance. It was one of the last stations to incorporate separate waiting facilities for ladies and gents. The main waiting room measured 81' by 30' (25m by 9m) and enjoyed a 12' (4m) high ceiling. The second floor was devoted entirely to divisional staff. The platform was constructed of brick and lit by a pair of ornamental iron light poles, each with a cluster of three lights.

From the station a landscaped park extended for one block west to Downie Street. Known as Station Park it was maintained by both railway and municipal employees, and was adorned with walkways, flower beds, hedges and flowering bushes. It was an era when most local stations could boast gardens. To provide plants to the local station agents, the GT added a green house to its Stratford complex, from which it shipped out more than 80,000 plants every spring. Another feature, found at a number of divisional stations across the country, was the railway YMCA.

But Stratford's railway days would not last. The greenhouse was removed in 1940. Between 1958 and 1964, the shops were drastically cut back and then eliminated altogether. Passenger service plummeted from 44 trains a day to seven. Today that number is a mere four. Soon the grand station began to deteriorate as CN removed both the tower and the gable and replaced the slate roof with asphalt shingles.

In 1989 VIA Rail upgraded the station, replacing the heating, the doors and windows and the ticket office. Unfortunately, they also chose to replace the lighting, and amid howls of protest, took away the ornamental light standards from the platform.

Today Stratford has become internationally known for its annual Shakespearean Festival, which commenced in 1954. Sadly, its legacy as a railway town has at the same time been largely forgotten. Still, the station gardens are carefully tended, and the building remains one of the finest stations in southwestern Ontario.

The station is located on Shakespeare Street between Front and Downie. The main part of town lies about 10 blocks north and is marked by its landscaped gardens along the Avon River, and the main street with its many shops, fine restaurants, and dramatic town hall.

An early drawing depicts a more elaborate plan for the Stratford station than was eventually constructed.

SUDBURY
A Legacy Overshadowed

Overshadowed by international and occasionally controversial reputation as a nickel mining and refining centre, Sudbury remains a major railway town. In the heart of its downtown core lies one of northern Ontario's most extensive railway yards. Beside them is the diminutive but pleasing historic CP station.

Sudbury even began its existence as a railway junction. After the CPR had built its line to Algoma Mills, as part of a proposed transcontinental route through the U.S., the government of Canada changed to an all-Canadian route. Sudbury Junction became the point at which the two routes joined.

Sudbury's original station was a simple plan nicknamed the "Van Horne" after the railway's builder.

While the bedrock was being blasted away for the new line, extensive deposits of copper were discovered. Later on, the nickel contained in them turned the area around the railway point into one of Canada's major mining centres. It has also remained an important CPR divisional point.

The stone and brick station was not the first to exist on the site. That was a simple standard wooden building designed as a "Van Horne" station, a plan being used for thousands of stations across the new CPR. As profits increased, however, most of these were replaced by more attractive and solid buildings.

Following the completion of yet another line in 1906, one linking Sudbury with Toronto, the yard became even busier, and a new station was built. Completed in 1907, it was one of forty new stations which the CPR built in Ontario to replace the aging wooden stock.

Because the divisional offices were in a separate building, which still stands, the passenger station did not need to be large. But it did need to be appealing. Using the chateauesque style typical of the period, the building incorporated a steep ski slope roof with a dormer for the agent's sleeping quarters puncturing the roof line. The solid station was built of brick on a stone foundation. Stations built in a similar style appeared at Bolton, Alliston, MacTier, Ignace and Mattawa, although these were all wood. Only that at Mattawa remains in situ, although there are plans to move it as well.

Originally the station contained a restaurant, a feature common to stations at divisional points. It was at these locations that trains would wait for 20 minutes or so while the engines were serviced, the coal tenders refilled with coal and the crews changed shifts. This would allow passengers a few moments for a quick light meal. In 1942 the station was upgraded to accommodate increasing traffic. More recent renovations have resulted in drop ceilings, flourescent lighting and the removal of the restaurant. The agent's quarters were closed off and the little dormer removed. The covering of grey paint was also removed to reveal the original brick and stone.

Until 1990, VIA Rail's popular *Canadian* would call here each day and split or assemble its Montreal and Toronto sections, depending upon direction.

However, in 1990, the government of Brian Mulroney slashed the *Canadian* service by half, eliminating the Montreal section entirely, and rerouting the train onto the less convenient and less scenic CN line. Since then, train service at the historic station consists only of the thrice weekly dayliner service to White River.

Sudbury's entire downtown grew around the railway yards. Elgin Street, which parallels the tracks, was lined with hotels and cafes to serve travellers and crew. Sadly, Sudbury's downtown has suffered from demolition of historic buildings and competition from suburban malls. Elgin Street has turned into a tawdry collection of bars and closed stores, while the station is surrounded by an unattractive parking area. Still, the building stands out as a visual gem in an otherwise unexceptional downtown landscape.

The CP offices beside the station have not been similarly upgraded, but remain a busy component of Sudbury's railway heritage.

VIA's trains to White River offer riders a unique cross-section of northern Ontario's lakelands and historic railway towns. Places like Cartier, Biscotasing and Chapleau all owe their existence to the arrival of the CPR. Other places like Lochalsh, a former gold mining town, and Nicholson, a once busy sawmill town, have become ghost towns. It's almost a journey which relives the railroading of another time. And it all begins at the Sudbury station.

The station sits on Elgin Street just west of Paris Street which is the city's main road in from the Trans Canada Highway.

The Sudbury station following restoration.

THUNDER BAY
Where the West Began

Within the sprawling urban area that is today Thunder Bay, it is difficult to locate much of its railway heritage. But it is there. And that is fitting because, in the story of Canada's railway history, Thunder Bay is where the west began.

The ground breaking for Canada's first transcontinental rail line took place, not in eastern Canada, but on the banks of the Kaministiquia River, a short distance upstream from a Northwestern fur trading post named Fort William. A small townsite appeared, its streets laid out in a grid typical of Canada's early railway towns. Its name was Westfort. Sorting yards stretched from the station to the grain elevator. The small wooden station was a two-storey structure with a hip gable end above

VIA Rail's Canadian makes one of its last stops at the Fort William "union" station.

the track side. Tracks were laid from the station to Canada's two coasts and along them the first train came through in 1886.

However, the shifting sands of the river created headaches for the ships' captains and newer elevators were built closer to the lake. With the rapid growth in the grain trade, new yards were established and another station built closer to the new yards, this one a full two storeys, built of wood, with double dormers in the roof. Again, a grid network of streets was laid in railway fashion behind the building.

By now the yards had obliterated the old fur trading post leaving only the stone munitions building. But it, too, was demolished shortly thereafter.

As settlement spread in Canada's west, two more transcontinental lines were added, the Canadian Northern, which added a large station in Fort William's rival town, Port Arthur, and the Grand Trunk Pacific which was laid out much further to the north. However, in order to bring its grain to the great lakes, the GTP established a branch line from a point east of Sioux Lookout to Fort William where it was proposed they share a station with the CPR.

With Fort William's importance as a grain port ever growing, the CPR added still more yard space and elevator capacity. In 1910 the CP and GTP opened their new $100,000 union station.

Its flat roof was a departure from the station styles of an earlier era, and resembled the station built in Regina about the same time. When finished, the station stood three stories with wings of a single storey extending from each end. The street entrance was distinguished by a two storey arch, outlined in stone above the main door. In fact the stonework spread right to the roof in a wide column which took in three windows on the third floor. Stone sheaves of wheat flanked the entrance. A clock was set in intricate wood latticework just above the door.

The front was further divided vertically by another pair of stone columns and corners which extended slightly beyond the full facade. Decorative stone trim extended around the roof immediately above the third floor windows.

The track side, by contrast, was relatively simple.

The interior consisted of a general waiting room which was 72' by 32' (22m by 10m). Just off the main room was the ladies' waiting room. A joint telegraph and ticket office, shared by the two companies, occupied the rest of the main floor. The offices of the two railway companies occupied the second and third floors. A lunch counter and newsstand were added to the station in 1921.

For most of its existence, Thunder Bay, now incorporating the former cities of Fort William and Port Arthur, has been Canada's largest grain port.

The economic and physical landscape of the lakehead has changed dramatically in recent years. Grain shipping has fallen drastically, and many of the elevators have been ripped away. Thunder Bay has over the last three decades increasingly become a multi-faceted city with shopping malls, a major university and sports and tourist facilities. Meanwhile the railways have slipped in significance. This was sadly underlined in 1990 when the federal government of Prime Minister Brian Mulroney eliminated the city's entire rail passenger service. Today, Fort William's union station is the city's last active railway station, but offers no passenger service.

The original station at Fort William.

TORONTO

NORTH TORONTO: The Booze Stop

Today, most of North Toronto's residents would know it as the Summerhill Liquor Store, and these likely are aware that it was once a railway station. But how many would realize that the stone building with the tall clock tower was once Toronto's other "union" station.

In 1884 the Ontario and Quebec Railway, later leased to the CPR, built a line across what was then the northern limits of Toronto, and located a small brick station beside Yonge St, naming it after the nearest village, Yorkville. By 1912 the CPR was also using the increasing-

CPR's effort at operating a rival union station at North Toronto was short-lived. The station closed after just 15 years of operation, although it did witness a Royal visit.

ly congested station built in 1873 by the Grand Trunk on Front St, and was growing impatient with the lack of progress on the construction of a new union station at that location. Their new overnight service to Montreal and a new train to Ottawa required more space.

To help ease the anticipated increase in traffic, and to attract more passengers to their rail line, the CPR proposed a union station of their own, to be shared with the Canadian Northern Railway. They hired the firm of Darling and Pearson, whose work included the Royal Ontario Museum and the Peace Tower in Ottawa, to design the new building.

Work started on September 9, 1915, ironically just two weeks before ground was broken for the new union station on Front Street. However, the work was completed in less than a year, a contrast to the more than 12 years required to eventually finish the Front Street station. Soon trains were departing for Ottawa, Montreal, Lindsay, Peterborough, Port Hope, Streetsville and Teeswater.

As had been the trend for the previous two decades, the tower played a major role in the station design. Rising 140' (45m) above Yonge St., the new station's tower became a North Toronto landmark. The station was flat roofed, with three large arched windows lighting the three storey waiting room. A metal canopy extended around the south and west sides of the building. Between the windows were railway-themed freizes.

Inside, the waiting room walls were covered with beige and green marble, while the ceiling displayed a dentil cornice. The floor was a basket weave terrazzo.

Because the tracks had been elevated along the route, the platforms were one level above that of the waiting room.

By 1930 the Canadian Northern had been absorbed by the Canadian National which was using the Front Street station, and usage of the North Toronto station dwindled to 20 trains a day. Because the new union station on Front Street was now fully operational, the CPR decided to close North Toronto, and run all their trains through the new station. On September 27, 1930, the station was closed and a year later it was the site of a beer store.

The former station was to be reopened, however. In 1939 King George VI and Queen Elizabeth, now the Queen Mother, were in the midst of their famous cross-Canada tour and planned to disembark at North Toronto from where a motorcade would carry them downtown. To do this it was necessary to reopen the building as a station for that day. On May 22 the train stopped, the King and Queen stepped out and a royal salute was fired. The motorcade eased off down Yonge St, and the next day the station resumed its role as a beer store. A year later it would also become a liquor store.

Sadly the renovations needed to sell liquor meant that the magnificent ceiling and walls were covered, and the waiting room partitioned off. By 1950 the broken clock with its 8-foot hands had also been removed.

In 1992 the station was designated as a heritage station under the HRSPA. Plans to redevelop the area around the station as condominiums include the restoration of the station itself. When it is refurbished the full glory of the mammoth waiting room will once more be revealed. The station is on the east side of Yonge Street three blocks south of St Clair Avenue, and is directly opposite the Summerhill subway station.

Passengers line up for tickets in the marble-walled waiting room in the North Toronto CPR station.

TORONTO'S UNION STATION
A Railway Cathedral

It may seem incongruous now that one of North America's grandest and most fully functional railway stations would have been the butt of jokes for so many years. However, the seemingly endless delays which plagued the construction of Toronto's magnificent Union Station so frustrated the local populace that it warranted the sarcasm.

The original plans for Toronto's waterfront were for a lakeside walkway and park beside which would be the institutions of the day and the grand homes of the gentry who ran them. But in the 1850s the railways had other plans. Ontario's first railway, the Ontario Simcoe and Huron, began its line from a shed-like station near what

The entrance to the departures platform.

The Front Street facade of the Toronto Union Station

is today Front and York. But the twin arrival of the Great Western Railway from the west and the Grand Trunk from the east finished the waterfront park.

The first union station was erected by the Grand Trunk in 1855 and shared by the Great Western. It stood at the corner of Bay and Front, but was temporary at best, and was replaced with a larger structure just three years later. In 1866 the Great Western built a station of its own at the corner of Yonge and the Esplanade, a building noted for its curved train shed. It survived until 1952, serving as a fruit market, until it burned.

For several years, the Toronto waterfront was a smokey mishmash of competing railway lines, each with its own station. The Northern Railway, a new name for the OSH, had stations at Spadina and at West Market Street beside what is today the St Lawrence Market. The Toronto and Nipissing added their station at the foot of Berkeley Street in 1869.

Then in 1873, when the Grand Trunk replaced its old wooden depot with the grandest station of the day, most of the other lines moved in as well, including the CPR in 1887. The long brick station overlooking the water consisted of a three-track train shed dominated by a trio of handsome domes. Toronto was a rapidly growing city and within just two decades the new union station was already inadequate. New tracks and a train shed were added to the waterside, obliterating the facade of the building. Meanwhile, on the city side, a major expansion was added on Front Street. But even with these additions, the station remained congested and the city began looking for a new location.

Toronto, meanwhile, was paying the price for its railway prosperity. With several tracks along the lake, access to the Toronto Island ferries was frequently blocked for extended periods. Finally, in 1892, a bridge was constructed over the tracks. Then on April 19, 1904, a fire which started in the E and S Currie factory at Wellington and Bay quickly spread through downtown Toronto. Fanned by a strong northwest wind, the inferno destroyed 122 buildings covering 14 acres.

And it was on part of this charred land that a new station would eventually arise. But just how "eventually" was not foreseen.

In 1906 the Toronto Terminals Railway was created to undertake the construction of the new station. In 1907 two sets of plans were submitted, one for a stub station and one for a through station. In 1909 the through station was chosen. Unable to wait for the new building, the CPR began construction of a union station of its own, north on Yonge Street near Summerhill which it would briefly share with the Canadian Northern Railway.

Then, in 1914, the firms of Ross and Macdonald and H.G Jones, along with architect John M. Lyle, were hired to create what would later be considered one the finest surviving grand stations on the continent. The design marked the new age in station building. Gone were the towers of the 1890s, and the steeply pitched roofs and ornamental gables of the Chateauesque era. Instead the emphasis was on the classical and the "city beautiful."

The 850 foot (250 m) long structure had as its most captivating exterior feature a colonnade of ten pillars stretching three storeys high, with four more on each side projecting over a pair of entrance porches. These were flanked in turn by two extensive wings, each of which ended with their own arched entrances three stories high.

The "city beautiful" aspect involved the proposal for a grand boulevard which would lead to the station from a city hall complex on Queen Street to the north. While the boulevard was never realized, the building was set back from Front Street a full 75 feet (25 m) to ensure that the grandeur of the building could be fully appreciated. Traffic was kept away by means of a sunken driveway accessed from the two side streets, Bay and York.

But the most spectacular feature would be the waiting room. Built on a scale that was reminiscent of New York's Pennsylvania Station, it soon came to be called the Grand Hall and was deliberately designed after the 5th century cathedral, the Santa Maria Maggiore in Rome. It was also marked with arches at each end, and another pair of pillars over the ramp to the tracks. Intricate ceiling work and the names of the railways' major destinations drew the eye high above. Washrooms and a restaurant would be located at the west end, while a small number of shops would group around the ramps. A bevy of ticket booths lined the wall on the south side and a circular information counter, with a clock, stood in the centre.

Functionality was not overlooked. Arriving passengers followed separate corridors from those who were embarking. While the latter could enjoy the enormity of the Grand Hall, those arriving were led directly to the street by means of underground corridors and ramps, without ever seeing the spectacular concourse.

But a decade and a half would pass before the public was able to use it. Construction lasted until 1920 when the railway companies were able to move into the offices. But the new elevated tracks were not down yet, and passengers were required to use temporary platforms beside the old tracks. The delay stemmed from a dispute over the construction of the large viaduct east of the station which would carry the tracks above most of the north-south streets and eventually over the Don River. Meetings, studies, delegations, and even a lawsuit by the Harbour Commission, dragged the planning process out for another five years.

Anger over the delay was often expressed in the form of sarcastic jokes heard on radio and in the vaudeville theatres.

Finally, by 1926, the plans for the viaduct were approved and construction of the final phase of the station, the concourse, could begin. On August 6, 1927, the Prince of Wales officially opened the station. It had taken 13 years to build; the ceremony lasted 11 minutes. Then, in October, demolition of the old union station began.

Many other features accompanied the building of the new facility. The CN added a new roundhouse near Bathurst, while the CPR built one of their own at the foot of John. The Royal York Hotel was built across the road and was connected by a tunnel beneath the street. A customs and express building, designed to complement the station, was constructed east of the station. Among the busiest stations in North America, Union Station would see the arrival and departure of more than 200 trains a day.

In 1970 the remarkable building was, incredibly, threatened with demolition. But the citizens of the city were not about to let that happen, and, led by a group which included Pierre Berton, Mike Filey and Peter Martin Associates, they rallied to save the station.

The original facade of Toronto's earlier union station was later obliterated to enlarge the outdated building.

With the inauguration of GO Train service, the east end of the basement was opened to link with the subway system and allow travellers to walk right through to the GO Train platforms. VIA Rail users, meanwhile, continued to use the Grand Hall. With the construction of the CN Tower, the Metro Convention Centre and the Sky Dome hotel and sports field during the 1970s and 80s, an enclosed skywalk was built to link the west end of the station with these various facilities.

With the redevelopment of the rail lands west of the station in the 1990s, most of the yards of the CPR and the CNR were removed, as were the various railway buildings, including the CN roundhouse, the coach house and the cabins. The CPR roundhouse was saved, although plans to convert it to a museum were killed by a penurious city council, and a brew pub now occupies part of the building. A pair of yard cabins were rescued from Bathurst Street and now stand unused beside the roundhouse. The CPR express building was demolished in 2001. The only vestige of Toronto's earlier station heritage rests in the name "Station St" which runs west from York Street opposite the west end of the current station.

Then, in November of 2001, the federal government announced that more than $10 million would be set aside to upgrade the station. At the same ceremony, the transport minister, David Collenette, unveiled new engines, new coaches, and announced additions to VIA Rail's passenger service. It is fitting that a new era in Canadian rail travel started in Canada's grandest station.

Around the time that preservationists were fighting to save Union Station, Toronto could still count nearly two dozen local stations. These included a pair at Parkdale, two at West Toronto, St Clair West, Sunnyside, Don, Main Street, Scarborough Junction, Agincourt, and Oriole, among several others. But while the fight for Union Station went on, the little stations gradually disappeared. Many burned, others were demolished. While a small station at Rexdale serves as a storage shed, and that at Mimico is in a state of near ruin, only the two "union" stations stand to recount Toronto's railway station legacy.

UNIONVILLE

A Farm Village in the City

Despite having been utterly overwhelmed by the urban sprawl of the Greater Toronto Area, the village of Unionville has survived largely intact, and the station landscape is a key part of it.

When William Gooderham first proposed a railway to the northeast of Toronto, it originated at his massive limestone distillery east of Toronto's Parliament St, and was planned to lead right to Lake Nipissing. In fact the line was never even surveyed that distance and terminated instead at Coboconk.

Anxious to get his line up and running, Gooderham built only very simple wooden stations. Most were single storey with a low unembellished roof line and the interiors were divided into the three standard functions of passenger, office and baggage. A number even lacked the operator's bay window. While most of the first generation stations were demolished or replaced, that at Unionville has survived. What makes this even more outstanding is that it was one of the simplest stations on the line and had to contend with another nearby station in Markham.

A view of the simple Unionville station when trains still called.

When the line was built in 1871, it had a significant impact on the urban shape of the little mill village. At that time, most of the village lay north of what would be the roadbed. But after the station was constructed, new growth occurred south of the station. Here the homes were grander and made of brick, while the simpler and older homes were wood.

A number of railway buildings appeared by the station, including the Stiver feed mills, the Dominion Wood and Coal elevators, an agent's house, stock yard and section tool house. But truck and car traffic exacted the usual price on the railway, and passenger service to Coboconk ended in 1955, freight service 10 years later. Eventually all rail was lifted from Coboconk to Uxbridge.

However, the line's railway era has not died. While the York and Durham heritage railway operates a popular tourist train from Stouffville to the restored station at Uxbridge, GO Transit runs commuter trains to Stouffville. For a time, one of the GO stops was directly opposite the Unionville station.

In 1982 CN, which still owned the station, indicated its intention to demolish the building. But the residents of the village loved their diminutive little station and rallied to save it. In 1989 the Town of Markham purchased the building and restored it for use as a community centre. In upgrading the building for its new use, the Town saved as many of the internal surface features as possible, although a new kitchen and washrooms were added. More recently the Town also acquired the historic Stiver mill which will be restored by a private entrepreneur as part of a commercial development.

Unionville remains a delight to visit, and is a popular destination for visitors from throughout the GTA. Its main street has changed little in appearance in a century thanks to the planners who have diverted the new roads around the village. It is an oasis of history amid the tedium of the sprawl which surrounds it, and at its heart is the old station.

The station stands on the west side of the main street at the south end of the business section, all of which is situated north of Highway 7 and west of Kennedy Road.

WHITE RIVER
Winnie's Railway Town

The town of White River and its original station enjoy a rare, and even unique status among Ontario heritage stations.

Located halfway between Thunder Bay and Sudbury, White River was right in the middle of what was called the "thousand mile gap," a stretch of undeveloped rock and forest. When the site was chosen for a divisional point, CPR not only created the town, but ran it.

The original station in this remote railway town was an elongated version of the CPR's commonplace plan.

Virtually everyone worked for the CPR. While the company houses were originally located west of the yards and opposite the station, a new townsite was laid out behind the station. The only facility for which the residents paid taxes was the school. Outside of that the CPR provided water and electricity, maintained the streets, and provided the houses. Community facilities were provided by the railway YMCA. Surprisingly, despite the virtual absence of agriculture in the area, White River contained the largest cattle yards between Winnipeg and Toronto. Up to 100 cattle cars would be parked in the yard at any one time, while the cattle were being exercised and fed.

The original station was a simple two-storey wooden structure which was simply extended every time a new function was added, until by 1914 it stretched twice its original length. It was also in that year that White River gained what would years later become its main claim to fame. As a troop train stopped for the requisite 20 minutes, a young army veterinarian saw on the platform a hunter holding a bear cub. Captain Harry Colbourne bought the bear as a mascot for his regiment, naming it after his adopted home town, Winnipeg.

As the bear became friendlier with the troops, it was nicknamed Winnie. When he went to the front, Colbourne gave the bear to the London Zoo where a young boy named Christopher Robin Milne became so fascinated with the furry creature, as did most of the children, that it inspired his father, the children's author A.A. Milne, to create a series of books. And so was born Winnie-the-Pooh. After overcoming initial objections from the owner of the Winnie copyright, the Disney Corporation, the town placed a Pooh carving in its tourist park.

With the building of the Trans Canada Highway in the 1950s, the town began to change. New commercial operations moved from the street behind the station to the new highway. The railway conceded the operation of the town to an elected municipal council, and sold most of its housing to their occupants. And it built a new station.

In 1947 the railway had already added a new two storey brick communication building, for this location was a major CP transmission point. Then, in 1957, it added a new station to the east end of that building. The station was designed in the railway's bold new post war modernist style, its single storey typified by a flat roof and rounded corners. Being at a divisional point, the station also contained a restaurant in the east end of the building.

In White River many of the old company houses still stand, several sporting their original red and yellow CPR paint scheme. The railway doctor's house is the most prominent of the lot. It stands on a hill east of the station and is a locally designated heritage property.

Although through passenger service ended with the cuts by the Mulroney government in 1990, the station continues its role as the terminus for the wilderness route of VIA Rail's thrice weekly Sudbury-White River train.

The station, a modernistic style, is attached to the end of the White River communications building.

WOODSTOCK
Ontario's Prettiest Station

One look at the old Woodstock station will convince the viewer that it may be one of the most fanciful small town stations in southern Ontario. Designed by the inveterate Great Western architect, Joseph Hobson, it was considered stylistically as a cross between Gothic and Italianate. Two storeys in height, several hip gables dominated the roof line, as well as picturesque angled surfaces and curving lines. For the walls Hobson used red brick, with white brick interspersed in vertical bands.

An early view of train time before the Great Western station at Woodstock was restored

The station displayed wide eaves and a large verandah supported by verge board and bracket designs against the walls. Its eight gables and peaks were crowned with eight-sided finials. Inside was a single large general waiting room with a baggage and customs room situated in separate buildings to the west of the main building. All three were connected by a canopy, later filled in, which gave the complex a gangly, extended look.

Although Hobson designed many other fine stations such as those at Sarnia, Hamilton and Chatham, the station at Woodstock was his most eclectic.

It was also one of the last to incorporate accommodation for the agent and his family. A kitchen and dining area were located on the ground floor on the southeast side of the buildings, while four bedrooms were located upstairs. Although Woodstock had ample housing, most of it was still on the north side of the tracks, while the station was on the south.

The station was built in 1882 and replaced a small wooden depot which was situated on the north side of the tracks. However, the Grand Trunk wished the north side to be reserved for factories, which had by then begun to line the tracks there, and located its new facility on the opposite side. The new site made it more accessible to rural travellers arriving from the farmlands that lay to the south.

Because the town had attained much of its developed form by the time the railways arrived, the location of the station had minimal impact on the shape of Woodstock's growth. From its beginnings as a planned town on Dundas Street in the 1790s, Woodstock grew to acquire more than 2000 residents and a new status as county seat before any of the railways reached town.

The first was the Great Western Railway with its Niagara Falls to Windsor line in 1854. Then in the 1870s came two more, the Credit Valley Railway, with a direct link to Toronto, and the Port Dover and Lake Huron Railway which operated between Port Dover and Stratford.

When the CPR threatened to expand and take over the CVR, the

GT, which by 1882 had amalgamated with the GW, decided to construct a new facility at Woodstock, and hopefully drain away the CPR's potential customers. The scheme worked, in part because the CPR station was well to the west of the main part of town.

The CN continued to service the town and its factories until the 1970s when it moved its employees out. The station by then was covered in an uninspiring grey paint and languished in a poorly maintained state. All other railway buildings were removed, and the last section of spur line belonging to the former PDLH railway was lifted. The only non-railway building attracted to the area was the old Grand Trunk hotel, which still does its duty as a tavern.

Much care went into restoring the exterior of the attractive Great Western station in Woodstock.

Following VIA Rail's acquisition of the station in 1986, the town lobbied for its restoration and VIA obliged. In 1992, at a cost of $300,000, architect Patrick Coles went to work in an effort to both upgrade the facilities and restore its Edwardian flavour. While unable to uncover the original brick, he did call for a new two-tone paint scheme, white with green highlights. A small garden, rare around stations today, occupies part of the former garden area. The building has once again become an attraction in this town of historic structures, and serves nine train arrivals each day, including the

VIA/Amtrak service to and from Chicago. The station is located on Henry Street between Bay and Wellington.

Woodstock is one of those rare places where both of its early stations still stand. Although not designated, the CPR station was built in the early 1900s and is a near copy of the stone and brick CPR station in Galt which was designated. Although run-down in appearance and much altered inside, the CPR station still functions as a yard office on what is a surprisingly busy route. This building can be found at the corner of Tecumseh Street and Ingersoll Avenue in the west end of town.

During restoration, the redundant freight shed was replaced with landscaping, right.

SELECTED BIBLIOGRAPHY

Andreae, Christopher, *Lines of Country, An Atlas of Railway and Waterway History in Canada*, (Cartography by Geoffrey Matthews, design by Mark Fram), Boston Mills Press, 1997,

Ballantyne, Bruce ed., *Canadian Railway Station Guide*, Bytown Railway Society, 1998,

Barnes, Michael, *Link With a Lonely Land; The Temiskaming and Northern Ontario Railway*, Boston Mills Press, 1985,

Bebout, Richard, ed., with John Taylor and Mike Filey, *The Open Gate; Toronto Union Station*, published by Peter Martin Assoc Ltd.,

Bohi, Charles, *Canadian National's Western Depots*, Fitzhenry and Whiteside, 1977,

Brown, Ron, *Ghost Railways of Ontario, Vols. One, and Two*, Polar Bear Press, 1998, 2000,

Brown, Ron, *The Train Doesn't Stop Here Any More; an Illustrated History of Railway Stations in Canada*, Lynx Images, 1997,

Canadian Heritage, *Parks Canada, Conservation and Change; The Heritage Railway Station Protection Act*, Minister of Supply and Services Canada, 1994,

Cooper Charles, *Narrow Gauge for Us*, Boston Mills Press,

Helm, Norman, *In the Shadow of Giants; the Story of the Toronto Hamilton and Buffalo Railway*, Boston Mills Press, 1978,

Jackson, John, and John Burtniak, *Railways in the Niagara Peninsula*, Mika publishing, Belleville, 1978,

Kalman, Harold, *A History of Canadian Architecture,* 2 vol, Oxford University Press, 1994,

Lavallée Omer, *Van Horne's Road*, Railfare, 1971,

Robinson, Dean, *Railway Stratford*, Boston Mills Press, 1989,

Smith, Mary, *Historical Background of the Grand Trunk Railway*, St Marys, <www.stonetown.com>,

Tennant, Robert D., *Canada Southern Country*, Boston Mills Press, 1991,

Township of Schreiber, *History of Schreiber; Canadian Pacific Railway*, <www.township,schreiber.on.ca>,

Wilmot, Elizabeth, *Faces and Places Along the Railway*, Gage Publishing, 1979,

Wilmot, Elizabeth, *Meet Me At the Station*, Gage Publishing,

Wilmot, Elizabeth, *When Any Time Was Train Time*, Boston Mills Press, 1992,

Wilson, Dale, *The Algoma Central Railway Story*, Nickel Belt Rails, 1984,

Wilson, Donald M., *The Ontario and Quebec Railway*, Mika Publishing, 1984,

Wilson, Ian, *Steam at Allandale*, Canadian Branchline Miniatures, 1998.

Unpublished Sources

Historic Sites and Monuments Board of Canada, *Railway Station Evaluation Reports*,

Ontario Ministry of Citizenship and Culture, *Planning for Heritage Railway Stations*, 3 vol, 1987,

Ontario Ministry of Transportation and Communications, Improving Rail and Intercity Bus Terminals in Small Municipalities, the Gravenhurst Experience, 1987,

Ontario Ministry of Transportation and Communications, *Orillia Railway Station Feasibility Study*, 1986,

Town of Cobalt, *Cobalt Railway Station Feasibility Study*, 1985.

<web.globalserve.net/~robkath/index.htm> (an excellent website not just for Ontario stations, but for background on historic rail lines as well)